Die Minnesinger *by Reinmar von Zweter.*

# The Book
# of
# Courtly Love

*The Passionate Code of the Troubadours*

Andrea Hopkins

HarperSanFrancisco
*A Division of* HarperCollins*Publishers*

A Labyrinth Book

THE BOOK OF COURTLY LOVE: *The Passionate Code of the Troubadours.*
Copyright © 1994 Labyrinth Publishing (UK) Ltd
Text copyright © 1994 by Andrea Hopkins

HarperSanFrancisco
*A Division of* HarperCollins*Publishers*

The Book of Courtly Love:
The Passionate Code of the Troubadours was produced by Labyrinth Publishing (UK) Ltd

Printed and bound by Singapore National Printers. Art direction and design by Magda Valine.
Picture editor: Patricia McCarver.
FIRST U.S. EDITION

Library of Congress Cataloging-in-Publication Data
Hopkins, Andrea
    The book of courtly love: the passionate code of the troubadours
    / Andrea Hopkins. — 1st ed.
          p.      cm.
    Includes bibliographical references.
    ISBN 0-06-251115-7. — ISBN 0-06-251129-7 (pbk.)
    1. Courtly love in literature.          I.  Title.
    PN682.C6H67   1994
    808.81'9354'0902—dc20                              94-2926
                                                        CIP

------------------------------------------------------------------------
    94  95  96  97  98  L A B  10  9  8  7  6  5  4  3  2  1

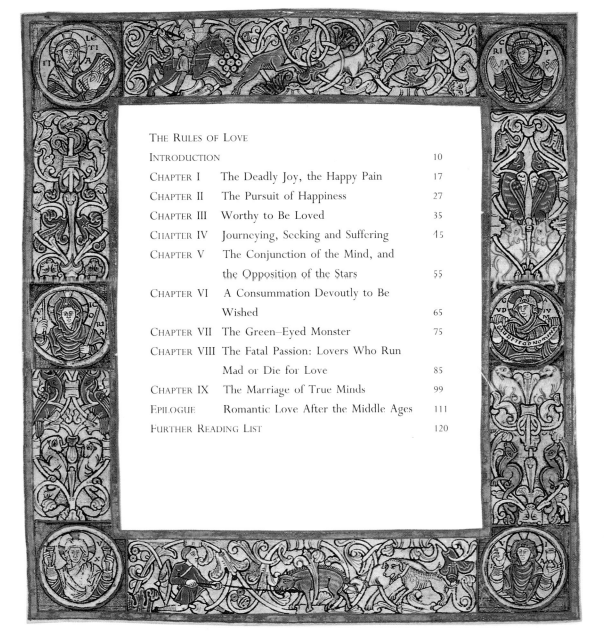

THE RULES OF LOVE

# The Rules

From Book II of *De Arte Honesti*

The state of marriage does not properly excuse anyone from loving. 1

He who does not feel jealousy is not capable of loving. 2

No one can love two people at the same time. 3

It is well-known that love is always either growing or declining. 4

Whatever a lover takes against his lover's will has no savor. 5

A male does not fall in love until he has reached full manhood. 6

A mourning period of two years for a deceased lover is required of the surviving partner. 7

No one should be prevented from loving except by reason of his own death. 8

No one can love unless they are compelled by the eloquence of love. 9

Love is accustomed to be an exile from the house of avarice. 10

It is unseemly to love anyone whom you would be ashamed to marry. 11

A true lover does not desire the passionate embraces of anyone else but his beloved. 12

Love that is made public rarely lasts. 13

Love easily obtained is of little value; difficulty in obtaining it makes it precious. 14

Every lover regularly turns pale in the presence of his beloved. 15

On suddenly catching sight of his beloved, the heart of the lover begins to palpitate. 16

# Of Love

*Amandi* by Andreas Capellanus.

17 A new love drives out the old.

18 A good character alone makes someone worthy of love.

19 If love lessens, it soon fails and rarely recovers.

20 A man in love is always fearful.

21 The feeling of love is always increased by true jealousy.

22 When a lover feels suspicious of his beloved, jealousy, and with it the sensation of love, are increased.

23 A man tormented by the thought of love eats and sleeps very little.

24 Everything a lover does ends in the thought of his beloved.

25 A true lover considers nothing good but what he thinks will please his beloved.

26 Love can deny nothing to love.

27 A lover cannot have too much of his beloved's consolations.

28 A small supposition compels a lover to suspect his beloved of doing wrong.

29 A man who is troubled by excessive lust does not usually love.

30 A true lover is continually and without interruption obsessed by the image of his beloved.

31 Nothing forbids one woman being loved by two men, or one man by two women.

From Book I of *De Arte Honesti Amandi* by Andreas Capellanus, (Dialogue 5).

1. Flee from avarice like a noxious plague, and embrace its opposite.
2. You must keep yourself chaste for your beloved's sake.
3. You must not deliberately try to break up a love affair between a woman suitably joined to another man.
4. Take care not to choose for your love a person whom a natural sense of shame would prohibit you from marrying.
5. At all costs take care to avoid lies.
6. Do not have many people in the secret of your love.
7. Being obedient in all things to the commands of ladies, always study to be enrolled in the service of love.
8. When fulfilling and receiving the pleasures of love, always let modesty be present.
9. Speak no evil.
10. Never publicly expose lovers.
11. Show yourself in all things polite and courteous.
12. When you are engaging in the pleasures of love, do not exceed the desires of your lover.

The Countess of Champagne was also asked what gifts it was fitting for ladies to accept from their lovers. To the person who asked this the Countess replied: "A lover may freely accept from her beloved these things: a handkerchief, a hair band, a circlet of gold or silver, a brooch for the breast, a mirror, a belt, a purse, a lace for clothes, a comb, cuffs, gloves, a ring, a little box of scent, a portrait, toiletries, little vases, trays, a standard as a keepsake of the lover, and, to speak more generally, a lady can accept from her love whatever small gift may be useful in the care of her person, or may look charming, or may remind her of her lover, provided however that in accepting the gift it is clear that she is acting quite without avarice."

*A tournament mêlée depicted in a late fourteenth century fresco at Castello Buonconsiglio, Trento, northern Italy. The knights exert themselves to show the ladies that they are worthy of love. The encounters of knights were not just training for real combat, but were also part of a ritual mating display.*

# Introduction

 OURTLY LOVE developed during the twelfth century in France, becoming an ideal of courtly society, both real and literary, throughout Europe for the rest of the Middle Ages. It celebrated an intensely idealized form of sexual passion—the kind of "falling in love" with which every society in every age is familiar—in a highly elaborate, sophisticated, and aristocratic code of behavior. It permanently influenced our culture and society, and the way we think about romantic love. This book explores and celebrates that code, at once breathtakingly alien and familiar.

Where did it come from? How did it start? The leisured classes of classical Roman society had enjoyed literature that celebrated love; but after the collapse of the Roman empire at the end of the fourth century, the life that permitted such refined enjoyments in France was largely swept away by successive waves of barbarian invaders. For centuries their society was illiterate; what survives of their poetry is grim martial epic, about war, blood-feuds, revenge, death; little concerned with women and love. But the south of France was different from the north. Separated by a different language (the *langue d'oc* in the south, the *langue d'oil* in the north), society was generally more stable here throughout the early Middle Ages than in the strife-torn north, and retained much more strongly the tastes and influences of Roman law and culture. Relative peace and prosperity, and continued contact with the much more sophisticated Arab society of Moorish Spain nurtured a civilized culture, based around the courts of the great nobles of Aquitaine, Auvergne and Poitou. At these courts, from the turn of the twelfth century onwards, were "troubadours" (literally "composers" or "finders") who combined the skills of poets, musicians, and singers. They were much more than just wandering minstrels: they were clever, witty, worldly, often highly educated and superbly skillful; they forged a whole new poetic diction, capable of great subtlety, complex abstraction and ingenious metaphor.

But it was more what they wrote about than how they wrote it that was so startlingly new. They wrote about love, and about the women they loved. In the poetry of the troubadours love was often celebrated in quasi religious terms, with the beloved woman being venerated as an object of worship, and much emphasis on the torments suffered by the lover. They invented a religious cult of love, with its own deities—Venus and Cupid—and its own temples, rites, prayers, priests and commandments. It was truly revolutionary because it placed women, who technically had no power in medieval society, in a position of complete dominance over their lovers. The beloved lady is the master, and the poet—even if in real life he was a great lord—is her servant, her humble supplicant. The poems express the poet's homage to his lady as if she were his feudal lord—often she is addressed as *midons,* a strange hybrid word containing the feminine version of "my" (*mia*) and the masculine noun for "lord" (*domnus*). The lady is not named, but is equally often clearly the wife of the poet's lord.

The goal aspired to in these love affairs is sometimes a platonic, spiritual union with the beloved, and sometimes a more physical one. We will probably never know how many, if any, of these literary love affairs were consummated in real life. On the face of it, for a poet to sleep with his lord's wife and then write poems about it would be incredibly dangerous. In a feudal society, where it was important for a lord to be sure that his heir had really been begotten by him, the greatest act of treason a vassal could commit was to sleep with his lord's wife. And yet it is clear from contemporary records that the writing of these love poems was seen to confer great "honor" and "worth" upon both the poet and the lady; this could mean, for the poet, status and money and patronage; and for the lady, status and fame. It was, in effect, an elaborate form of flattery. The adoration of noble ladies expressed the emotional and social aspirations of both the poets and their audience of courtly gentlemen and ladies.

The twelfth century was a time of massive social and cultural development, often referred to as a "Renaissance." The troubadours were quickly imitated in northern France (*trouveres*) and Germany (*minnesinger*). The courtly, sophisticated cult of love with its emphasis on emotion and suffering transformed the values of the existing aristocratic literature, epic *chansons de geste* (Old French epic poems which recounted the exploits of Charlemagne—or other noted leaders—and their knights), and was a decisive influence on the emergent literature of romance.

Romance narratives came in all shapes and sizes. A particular kind, known as Breton lays, were usually short, based on ancient Celtic tales and glittering with magical manifestations. They often featured non-human characters from the world of Faerie and told love stories. The most

famous writer of these lays was a woman poet, Marie de France. In her lays love is an irresistible power experienced equally by men and women; she frankly acknowledges the emotional needs and sexual appetites of her heroines.

Longer romances tended to focus on the character of the knight-hero. Perhaps the most important thing that distinguished it from previous epic literature was its emphasis on its characters' emotions, especially those of love. There was great appeal in the novel idea that relations between aristocratic men and women could be determined, not by the dynastic, territorial and financial imperatives which actually governed the marriages of feudal aristocracy, but by an irresistible passion experienced mutually and leading either to the enjoyment of supreme happiness, or the degradation of utter (and usually fatal) misery. One result of these romances' emphasis on the inner person, with his or her doubts, anxieties, conflicts and emotions, was to establish a tension between the idealism of love and war, between action and introspection. Chrétien de Troyes, greatest of the subsequent romance writers, gave much thought to working out a harmony between these two apparently conflicting forces. In romance literature the cultivation of refined and elevated emotions modified and civilized the warrior-hero into the courtier and gentleman. During the entire period of the Middle Ages this new concept of romantic love was seen and discussed as a humanizing and refining influence, a socially improving experience. Whereas the warrior-hero of an epic would typically fight to protect his lord, his comrades, or his society, the knight-hero of romance would perform his deeds to prove himself worthy of his lady, to improve himself, to achieve his full potential as a man and as a knight. For the first time in post-classical Europe a man's status as a civilized being, a member of courtly society, was judged partly by his behavior towards women. This is reflected in some of the romantic poems and tales of this period which survived and have been long admired.

By the later decades of the twelfth century the ethos of courtly love was codified and written down. In the first century B.C. the great Roman poet Ovid had composed his *Ars amatoria* (*The Art of Loving*). This was a collection of precepts illustrated by tales and legends intended (tongue in cheek) to instruct its readers in the arts by which men could seduce women. In the late twelfth century, probably between 1184 and 1186, this well-known literary classic was reinterpreted for modern times by one Andreas Capellanus—Andreas the Chaplain—in a Latin treatise called *De Arte Honesti Amandi* (*On the Art of Honorable Loving*). Andreas tells us that he was a chaplain in a royal household, but because he often mentions Countess Marie de Champagne (who, it is known, had a chaplain called André), and because his work is so close in spirit to the *Lancelot* of Chrétien de Troyes, which was written for Marie at about the same time, it has often been assumed that he worked at least for a while at the court of Champagne, and may have known Chrétien himself. At any rate, he was a member of a highly sophisticated courtly society, an educated, even learned man, and almost certainly in minor orders.

There are good grounds for believing that Andreas' book was intended as an elaborate intellectual joke. Andreas took over Ovid's theme of adulterous love, and subjected it to characteristically medieval methods of scholastic analysis. This resulted in outrageously distorted arguments and paradoxes—he stated, for example, that true love is not possible within marriage (because true love is impossible without jealousy and one cannot possibly be jealous of one's own spouse), and at the same time that true love (i.e. immoral love) is morally improving. Ovid quite frankly admitted that people "fell in love" as the result of strong sexual attraction; Andreas with mock solemnity looks on it as a spiritual exercise, almost a duty. His insistence that true love must be extramarital was taken quite seriously for a long

time as a prerequisite feature of courtly love.

Andreas tended to push the recognizable symptoms of desire to extremes. We know that people in the Middle Ages found his treatise screamingly funny, though it is hard to raise a chuckle out of it today. But, although we cannot take Andreas' rules absolutely seriously, we can take them largely so. A parody cannot

there are not more treatments of the correct behavior for lovers. From the *De Arte Honesti Amandi* it is clear that fashionable courtly society enjoyed debating the rights and wrongs of romantic love; that it loved tortuous moral dilemmas and twisted paradoxes; and that certain conventional forms of behavior had become sufficiently established and familiar by this time to be recognized and codified, even if in jest. The code existed, and was certainly developed in response to a need—the need to make sense of something potentially chaotic and destructive, to impose order on experience, and meaning on life. And it is not entirely without meaning for us, at the turn of the second millennium, to look at these glittering fragments and try to recreate the whole beautiful, crazy edifice of "courtly love" in all its exaggerated splendor, and to relate it to the powerful emotions at its foundation, which we still recognize and experience today.

*The tradition of musical entertainment was widespread. This charming early sixteenth century engraving shows a group of German musicians performing at a family dance at Augsburg.*

exist without the object that it parodies. There may even have been more serious codes of courtly love which have not survived; medieval people were very fond of codes and rules and lists of things, and among all the treatises and guides on chivalry, on hunting, on table manners, and other aspects of courtly life which have come down to us, it is only surprising that

When I see the lark fluttering
Its wings for joy against the sunbeam,
Until it reaches oblivion, and swoons
From the sweetness that pierces its heart,
Ah, such great envy seizes me
Of whatever I see rejoicing,
I marvel that this instant
My heart does not break with desire.

Alas, I thought I knew so much
Of love, and yet I know so little!
For I cannot stop myself loving her
From whom I shall never have joy.
My whole heart, and all of me from myself
She has taken, and her own self, and all the
world,
For when she took herself from me, she left me
nothing
But desire and a yearning heart.

I have never had power over myself,
Nor was I mine from that moment
When she let me look into her eyes,

Into a mirror that much pleases me.
Mirror, since I mirrored myself in you,
I have been slain by sighs from the depths,
And thus I was lost, just as
The fair Narcissus lost himself in the pool.

I despair of ladies;
I shall never trust them again,
And just as I once held them dear,
So I shall now hold them cheap.
Since I see that not one of them will help me
Against her who destroys and confounds me,
I doubt and disbelieve them all,
For well I know they are all like one another.

By this does my lady appear like a true woman,
And therefore I relate it of her,
For she does not want what a woman ought to
want,
And what she has been forbidden to do, she does.

**Bernard de Ventadour**

# CHAPTER ONE

## THE DEADLY JOY, THE HAPPY PAIN

LOVE at first sight has become something of a romantic cliché; nevertheless, it is based on something absolutely real—an instantaneous strong attraction to another person, not based on reason or knowledge, and yet much more meaningful than mere lust. Anyone who has been lucky enough to experience this—and countless numbers have if we are to believe the literature, music and film of today—knows that it really is possible to fall in love with someone the very first time we see them, and it is a phenomenon still widely celebrated in Western culture. There is truly something mystical in the sense of inner certainty we feel when this happens to us, despite the fact that we might have no real knowledge of the other person's character or feelings. This magical sense of suddenly perceiving a truth made medieval people feel that they had been attacked in some way by an external force—Love in person, shooting his arrows tipped with the irresistible drug of passion. Nowadays we tend to think of the magic as being a more abstract universal force, rather than a personification of love or a pagan god, but the existence of a magical certainty is still a valid and potent idea.

In the world of the courtly lover, love is always at first sight. Love's arrows strike the lover through the eyes, and travel straight to the heart, the moment the lover catches sight of the beloved. Andreas Capellanus is matter-of-fact about this moment:

> When a man sees a woman worthy of love, and with a pleasing figure, he immediately begins to desire her in his heart, and the more he thinks about her the more he burns with love, until she fills his mind the whole time.

In other words, instantaneous attraction leads directly to immoderate longing and obsessive love. Early romance writers had the same idea:

*Love aimed well when he shot his arrow into her heart—often she grew pale and broke into a sweat; in spite of herself she was forced to love.*

(Chrétien de Troyes, *Cligès*)

*Love herself had avenged her by striking Yvain such a gentle blow through the eyes into her heart.*

(Chrétien de Troyes, *Yvain*)

*Don't you see how Love has wounded me, flinging his arrow so that my whole heart is set ablaze? The arrow was poisoned; and I have been wounded in two places, because I received the blow that causes me such anguish both through the ear and the eye. There never was such a skilled archer as Love, who strikes so surely!*

(Anon, *Flamenca*)

war and locked up in a tower. Palamon first sees the beautiful Emilia as she gathers flowers in a garden beneath his cell:

*He cast his glance upon Emilia;*
*And straight he blenched and cried out, "Ah,"*
*As though he had been stung unto the heart.*
*And with that cry Arcite up did start*
*And said, "Cousin, what ails you,*
*That are so deathly pale to look upon?"*
*This Palamon answered and said again,*
*"Just now I took a hurt, via my eye*
*Into my heart, that will be the death of me.*
*The fairness of that lady that I see*
*Yond in the garden roaming to and fro*
*Is cause of all my crying and my woe."*

(Chaucer, *Knight's Tale*, ll 1074-1100)

Later writers elaborated the idea and we can see the process of the fatal first glimpse dramatized in Chaucer's *Knight's Tale*. Two cousins and sworn brothers, Palamon and Arcite, have been taken prisoner by Theseus in

*This exquisite illustration shows Emilia in her garden making herself a headdress from red and white roses while poor Palamon and Arcite gaze longingly from behind their prison bars. It was painted by the Master of the Hours of the Duke of Burgundy, c. 1465.*

And Chaucer puts it still more explicitly later on in his great love story *Troilus and Creseyde*, when Troilus first catches sight of Creseyde in the temple of Athena in Troy:

*And so it fell that, looking through the crowd,*
*His eye did penetrate, and went so deep,*
*That on Criseyde it struck, and there did keep.*

*And with that suddenly he felt as stunned.*
*And cautiously he stole a closer look.*
*"Ah, mercy, God," he thought, "where have you been,*
*Who are so fair and lovely to behold?"*
*With that his heart began to spread and rise;*
*He softly sighed, lest anyone should hear,*
*And caught again his normal jesting cheer.*

*… And from her look in him began to grow*
*Such great desire and passionate affection*
*That in the bottom of his heart did show*

*An image deeply fixed of her impression.*
*And though at first he'd gazed around the room,*
*His insolent horn began now in to shrink,*
*He scarcely knew whether to look or blink.*

(Chaucer, *Troilus and Criseyde*, Book I, ll 271-301)

Here we see that Troilus experiences the sense of recognition, and expresses it by the medieval equivalent of the modern cliché, "Where have you been all my life?" But in fact we have a new theory here—Chaucer is not using the image of Love shooting his arrows. The third stanza refers to a theory of vision dating back to ancient Greece and accepted by the philosopher Plato. According to this theory, the eye saw objects by transmitting a beam of light into them; therefore when glances met, an eye could send its beam through the eye of the beholder and could, as happens here, imprint the image of the beloved on the heart of the

lover—like striking an image onto a coin. Again, we have a strong sense of the body being invaded, attacked, penetrated; love is something that happens to you, something you have no control over.

Once the lover has seen the beloved and been smitten by love, he or she enters the next stage of the love affair, in which love is felt but not yet acknowledged. It is at this point that we encounter the most central proposition of the code of love—that love is suffering. In fact, Andreas Capellanus categorically defines it as just that:

*Love is a certain inborn suffering proceeding from the sight of and immoderate concentration on the beauty of the opposite sex, which makes each lover yearn above all else to enjoy the embraces of the other, and to fulfill by mutual desire all Love's commandments in each other's arms.*

The state of love is classically described as one of anguish and torment; but, in one of the paradoxes of which medieval people were so fond, it's a happy pain, one the sufferer would much rather endure than give up. This pain manifests itself in various ways, but is basically of two kinds—frustration and fear. The first kind concerns the physical symptoms of love, so tellingly described by Andreas in some of his Rules:

*Every lover regularly turns pale in the presence of his beloved. On suddenly catching sight of his beloved, the heart of the lover begins to palpitate. A man tormented by the thought of love eats and sleeps very little.*

The second source of pain is the mental anguish that besets the lover. Andreas explains that it is perfectly obvious that love is suffering, because anyone who loves is always beset by fear that their love will be unrequited—if a man is poor, he fears that his lady will reject him for his poverty; if he is ugly, that she is bound to love someone more handsome; if he is rich, that she will be revolted by his rapacious past. This time of doubt and uncertainty means for the lover the pain of insecurity, the fear of failure and rejection. To love is to open yourself to the risk of terrible hurt. Yet the literature of love insists that the lover is refined and ennobled by this suffering. To love is an exquisite pain and yet gives great joy; and even if it leads nowhere the lover would never give it up—witness these lines by the troubadour Arnaut Daniel:

> Every day I improve and grow better,
> For I serve and adore the noblest lady
> In the world—and I declare it openly.
> I am hers from head to foot;
> And, even if the cold winds blow,
> The love that is reigning within my heart
> Keeps me warm in the deepest winter ...
> I don't want the Empire of Rome,
> Or to be made Pope,
> If it meant that I could not return
> To her from whom my heart burns and cracks;

> And if she does not heal my suffering
> With a kiss before the end of the year
> She will murder me and damn herself.
> Yet for all the suffering I endure
> I do not renounce sweet love,
> Although it holds me in solitude
> And therefore I have fashioned these words in rhyme
> ... I am Arnaut, who gathers the wind,
> Who chases the hare with the ox,
> And swims against the tide.

Lovers who have not made their love known to the beloved, and who are not confident of it being reciprocated, however, are often in a still more pitiable plight. For example, the lovers Alexander and Soredamors in Chrétien de Troyes' *Cligès* suffer all the symptoms described by Andreas, because each is too shy to confess their love to the other:

> [Soredamors] paid dearly for her great haughtiness and scorn. Love has heated her a bath that greatly burns and scalds her...The queen took notice, and saw the two of them frequently flush, grow pale, sigh, and tremble... Love continually

*An early fifteenth century Italian tray depicting Lancelot and Tristan,*
*amongst others, as legendary lovers venerating Venus.*

*Troilus employs Criseyde's uncle Pandarus as a go-between in declaring
his love for her. This illustration from an early fifteenth century
manuscript shows Pandarus informing his niece of Troilus' love for her.*

*filled [Alexander's] mind with the one who had wounded him so deeply, for she tortured his heart and allowed him no rest in his bed... All night long [Soredamors] was in such great torment that she could neither rest nor sleep. Love had locked up within her body a conflict and frenzy that troubled her heart so that it nearly failed her, and that so tormented and obsessed her that she wept all the night through lamenting, tossing, and trembling.*

The same problems afflict Troilus after his fatal vision of Criseyde:

*And from then on Love robbed him of his sleep,*
*Made of his food his foe, and then his sorrow*
*Multiplied so that, if anyone took keep,*
*It showed in his complexion night and morrow....*
*But then poor Troilus suffered such great woe*
*That he went almost mad, for his fear went*
*That she already loved another so*
*That to his pains she'd be indifferent,*
*For which he felt his heart's blood almost spent;*

(Chaucer, *Troilus and Criseyde*, Book I, ll 484-490, 498-504)

These examples may seem extreme and far-fetched, they are only a slightly exaggerated and stylized version of sensations familiar to many people today. The sudden pallors, flushes, sweats and palpitations of the courtly lover recognizably yield to the modern reader the physical signs of strong sexual attraction. And although nowadays when people are accustomed to more direct communication and less restraint and it is much rarer for love to remain unacknowledged for long, it surely still happens that people loose sleep, toss and turn, experiencing the perilous thrills of unrequited love.

But delicious though these sensations may be, they cannot last forever; the lover is bound to try to achieve the fulfillment of love. And the next step is to confess it.

Sweet lady, that ring
That you gave me gives me great comfort
For by it my sorrow is lessened
And, when I look on it, I am more lighthearted
Than a starling;
And for your sake I am so brave,
I am not afraid that either lance nor arrow
Can do me harm, nor steel nor iron.
But on the other hand, I am in deeper despair
Through too much loving
Than a ship when it is tossed on the sea,
Distressed by waves and winds,
So terribly do my thoughts torment me.

Lady, just as when a castle
Is besieged by powerful lords,
When the catapult batters the towers,
And the balistas and the mangonels,
And so ferocious
Is the fighting on all sides
That neither tricks nor stratagems can help them,
And the pain and the screams are so dreadful
Of those inside who are in great agony:
Does it not seem to you
That they need to cry for mercy?

Thus I cry mercy of you, humbly,
My sweet, noble and worthy lady.

Lady, just as a lamb
Is powerless against a bear,
So I am, if your worth
Does not help me, weaker than a reed
And my life will be shorter
For it diminishes by a quarter
Whenever I take harm from the fact that
You do not put right for me what' is wrong.
And you, Fin'Amor, who protect me,
Who should guard
Noble lovers from folly,
May you protect and guide me
In the presence of my lady, since she so
vanquishes me.

Minstrel, with these new songs
Get you gone, and carry them into the presence
Of the beauty who brings forth greatness
And tell her that I am more hers
Than her own cloak!

Giraut de Borneil

# Chapter Two

## The Pursuit of Happiness

ANYONE who has fallen in love and is not yet loved in return suffers intense anguish. The courtly lover is not content to hug his secret to himself and, no matter how great his fear of rejection, is ultimately compelled to make known his love to the object of it. This is a dangerous time, fraught with difficulties. He may be paralyzed by shyness. If his beloved lady is far above him socially, he may actually have physical difficulty in getting close to her to confess his feelings. Or he may be physically incapacitated because the intensity of his feelings have made him ill.

Nevertheless, he must try. Thus Guigemar, hero of one of the Breton lays of Marie de France, bravely attempts to convey to his chosen love the depth of his feelings for her:

*Whoever can find a constant lover, he must love her and serve her to the utmost, and be completely at her will. Guigemar loved in the extreme: but he*

*swiftly received help, that he should not have to go on living contrary to his wishes. Love granted him courage, so that he revealed to her his heart's desire.*

*"Lady," said he, "I die for your love. My heart is in agony from it, and if you are unwilling to heal me, then it will be the death of me in the end. I require of you your love; fair one, do not deny me!*

(Marie de France, *Guigemar*, ll 493-506)

In this particular instance Guigemar is lucky, for his direct approach succeeds with his lady, not least because she has fallen equally in love with him. But, alas, this much desired outcome does not always ensue. In the romance *Guy of Warwick*, the hero falls in love with the daughter of an Earl; he is only a lowly squire, the son of the Earl's steward. Guy, despite being terrified of Felice's superior rank, and the thought that she might betray his presumptuous announcement to her father, is nevertheless compelled to risk everything to reveal his love:

> *Guy took himself into the court*
> *Like one whom woe has overwrought,*
> *And flung himself upon his knees*
> *Right there before the fair Felice ...*
> *And said, "Felice the fair, mercy!*
> *For God's love and that of Our Lady,*
> *Let me not find you still my foe,*
> *But listen to me, I beg of you ...*
> *Above all others I must love thee,*
> *Whether life or death's in store for me ...*
> *Unless you have mercy on me today,*
> *For sorrow I shall myself soon slay;*
> *But if you knew the heavy grief,*
> *The sorrow and pain beyond belief,*
> *That I have suffered both night and day—*
> *True love compels me this to say—*
> *If your own eyes my grief could see,*
> *You surely would have pity on me."*

(Anon, *Guy of Warwick*, ll 341-376)

Unfortunately Felice pours the cold water of common sense onto the bonfire of Guy's passion, and tells him to leave at once before she tells her father. Guy departs with his tail between his legs, only to suffer more sleepless and tormented nights. He returns, however, to declare that he does not care whether she tells her father or not; death would be welcome after such sufferings as he has endured. Thereupon, as if on cue, he promptly faints. Felice begins to look more kindly on him; to realize that, even if he is not of noble birth, he possesses qualities which may make him a suitable match for her. But we see here a perfect expression of the emotional blackmail so often employed by the stricken lover—I'm wounded, I'm in pain, I'm suffering, and all because of you; if you don't relent I shall die, and you will have killed me. This was a technique employed to even greater effect by that essential adjunct to medieval love affairs, the go-between. It often happened that the lover had not the courage or the opportunity to

*In Henry Thomas Schafer's* A Time of Roses, *a young gallant of the Italian Renaissance plays love songs to his lady. Her relaxed, dreamy demeanor implies either that he is her accepted lover, or that she is unaware of his feelings for her.*

approach the beloved lady himself; and then, despite the urgent necessity for secrecy, it was an accepted practice to use go-betweens, right from the earliest days of the troubadours. A lover would employ a troubadour to speak for him to the lady. Here is a *tenson* (poetic dialogue) by two anonymous *trobairitz* (female troubadours), one a married lady and one a *donzela* (or maiden) who, in this case, has been chosen as a go-between by the suitor of the married lady.

*Andreas Capellanus said that monks ought to abstain from the delights of the flesh. However as they were often overfed and underemployed, they often succumbed. Here a monk has been put in the stocks with his mistress.*

> *Good lady, you have such great courage,*
> *That I can't stop myself from counseling you:*
> *And I tell you that you are doing a great villainy,*
> *For you are letting this man who has never loved*
> *Anyone so much, die; and you don't know why;*
> *And if he dies, you will have the blame,*
> *For he will see no other lady but you alone,*
> *And you alone have power and mastery over him...*

> *If he desires my love, damsel, he must show*
> *A bold face, and be gay and full of worth,*

> *Frank and humble, not striving with any man,*
> *And have a courteous reply for everyone;*
> *For I don't want a proud or cruel man,*
> *Through whom my worth will be decreased or lost,*
> *But one who's frank and fair, discreet and amorous:*
> *If he wants me to treat him kindly, let him listen to my words.*

But we see the finest development of this technique in Chaucer's *Troilus and Criseyde*, in which Troilus' uncle Pandarus undertakes to inform Criseyde of Troilus's love for her. But he does much more than just inform her:

*"Now, my dear niece, our noble king's own son,*
*Good, wise, and worthy, frank of heart and true,*
*Noble Troilus, is so much in love with you,*
*That, if you help him not, he'll surely die.*
*Well, that is all! For what more can I say?*
*Do what you please, either to save or slay.*

*But if you let him die, I will not live—*
*This is the truth, niece, for I speak no lies—*
*I'll cut my throat at once, with my own knife!"*
*With that the tears came bursting from his eyes:*
*"And when we both lie dead, free from all guilt,*
*The thought of a fine catch you then can cherish:*
*What good does it do you if we both perish?*

*Alas, he that has been my lord so dear,*
*That faithful man, that gentle, noble knight,*
*Who asks for nothing but your friendly cheer*
*I watch him dying as he walks upright,*
*Hurrying out to battle day and night,*
*Seeking his death, if fortune send that duty.*
*Alas, that God bestowed on you such beauty!*

*For if it be that you so cruel prove*
*That no more care to you would be attached,*
*If death so true a gentleman remove,*
*Than would the end of some low, gambling wretch;*
*If you be such, your beauty shall not stretch*
*To make amends for such a cruel deed;*
*Better to be advised before there's need:*

*Woe to the gem whose beauty bears no force!*
*Woe to the herb that bears no healing shoot!*
*Woe to the beauty who feels no remorse!*
*Woe to the one that treads each underfoot!*
*And as for you, who are beauty's crop and root,*
*If in you there is not a drop of truth,*
*Then you were better dead, and that's the truth!"*

(Chaucer, *Troilus and Criseyde*, Book II, ll 316-350)

This is a technique cunningly designed to work in two ways. In the first place it created a sense of guilt and obligation in the lady. It is Criseyde's fault that Troilus is now dying of the pains of love for being so beautiful; and it is the duty of the possessors of such fatal beauty to be generous and kind to those who are smitten by it, or they stand accused of being like "the gem whose beauty has no force." (Gemstones, like crystals nowadays, were believed to have distinct powers.) In the second place, such an accusation is of course extremely flattering.

Andreas Capellanus is very much less "romantic" about the techniques a hopeful lover should employ to gain the affections of his lady. The first book of his treatise *De Arte Honesti Amandi* contains several dialogues between men and women, intended to demonstrate how a man of the bourgeoisie should woo a woman of his own class, of the gentry, and of the nobility; then how a gentleman should do it, and so on.

The dialogues themselves are tediously extended intellectual arguments, the object of which is unquestionably to persuade the woman into bed. For example, the dialogue between the gentleman and the bourgeoise opens with the gentleman asking her to judge whether a good character deserves more praise in a woman of noble birth or a woman of no blood or family. She answers, a woman of noble birth. He argues that this is wrong, because, just as we should think more highly of the skill of a craftsman who makes a good boat out of poor timber than out of fine timber, good character is more to be prized in those of humble birth. She concedes that certainly a good thing is prized more highly if it is also rare. He declares that he loves her for her excellent character. She replies that he ought not to seek the love of a woman outside his own class just because he cannot find anyone in it who is prepared to love him. He claims that love has compelled him to love her despite her birth, because of her beauty and character. She then uses his own argument against him, saying that he has just pointed out that it is better to love a person of humble birth with a good character, so why

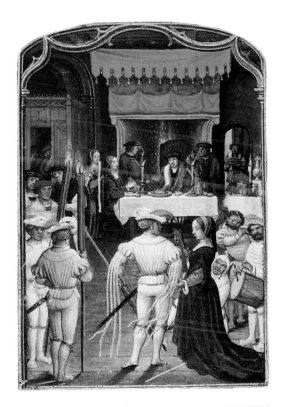

*This beautiful painting from the Hours of the Blessed Virgin, c. 1500, shows minstrels and mummers about to entertain a lord and his lady and their guests at a feast.*

should she love him rather than seek a man of good character in her own class? And so it goes on. In the end he resorts to the usual emotional blackmail—if she rejects him, he will die, and she will be his murderess. After a little more banter the charm of this statement takes effect:

She: *If you really propose to carry out what you have just claimed in words, it is certain that you will be abundantly rewarded, either by me or some other lady.*

He: *May God grant that your words express your true feelings; and as for me, though I may seem to be parted from you physically, yet in my heart I am forever bound to you.*

And this brings us nicely to the next stage in the progress of the love affair. The lover has fallen in love, he has declared his affections to the lady (or had someone else do it for him), and she has indicated her interest—now he must prove himself worthy of her love.

Courteously I want to begin
A verse, if there is anyone to listen to it,
And since I have gone into it thus far,
I will see if I can refine it,
For now I want to make my song pure,
And tell you about many things.

A man can certainly be vulgar
Who wishes to blame Courtliness,
Of whom the wisest and best taught man
Cannot say or do so much
But that a man would not be able to teach him
Something more, great or small, at some time.

He can boast of Courtliness
Who knows well how to keep Moderation;
And whoever wants to hear everything there is,
Or to gather up everything he sees,
Must keep Moderation in all his deeds,
Or else he will never be too courtly.
It is Moderation to speak quietly,
And it is Courtliness to love;

And he who does not wish to be despised
Should guard against all vulgarity,
Against mocking taunts and foolish behavior,
And if he does this, then he will be wise.

I want to send the verse and the tune
To my lord Jaufré Rudel in Outremer *
And I wish the French could hear it,
So as to lighten their hearts;
And may God grant them this:
Where there is sin, let there be mercy.

**Marcabrun**

* [i.e. "beyond the sea" - Jaufré had gone
on the second crusade].

# CHAPTER THREE

## WORTHY TO BE LOVED

THE medieval literature of courtly love showed a very highly developed sense of how a lover ought to behave in order to be worthy of his lady's affection. The lover was not seen as a distinct personality, but had to conform to a type; and his typical qualities were discretion, faithfulness, obsession, generosity, and courtesy.

Secrecy was an essential ingredient to the success of a love affair and all sources concur on this point. There is of course a practical reason for this—in many of the love affairs described in the poetry of the troubadours, in the romances, and certainly in Andreas Capellanus' treatise, one or other of the lovers was married to someone else; and in fact Andreas insisted that true love can only exist outside matrimony. However familiar and well-accepted this became as a literary convention, it remained very much outside the realms of acceptable public behavior

in a society dominated by the doctrines of the Church to a degree that is almost inconceivable today. But there are also medieval poems and tales which describe love affairs of blameless rectitude which end in marriage; and for them, too, secrecy is an expected norm. Andreas cites several rules on the subject:

(First set of rules, from Book I):

6. *You mustn't have many people in the secret of your love.*

9. *You ought not to speak evil of others.*

10. *You must never publicly expose lovers.*

(Second set of rules, from Book II):

13. *Love that is made public rarely lasts.*

Now, this is not really anything to do with the fear of getting caught in compromising circumstances with someone else's wife. It has more to do with love being essentially a private thing between lovers, a special private world which is very fragile and can all too easily be destroyed by the envy, cruelty, mockery and malicious gossip of the world at large. Elsewhere in his treatise Andreas points out that he does not approve of people falling in love with one another on the grounds of beauty alone, "because between incautious or less skillful lovers, love cannot be concealed for long, and therefore from the moment it begins, it has no idea how to increase. For, when love is divulged, it does not cause the lover to be well thought of, but instead usually brands his reputation with hurtful rumors, and in short does him a lot of damage" (*De Arte*, Book I, chapter VI). In Marie de France's Breton lay *Lanval*, the whole plot hinges on the hero's discretion. Sir Lanval, an impoverished knight of King Arthur's court, has the good luck to become the lover of a very rich faery lady, who has traveled from her own distant country to seek his love, having heard of his beauty and prowess. Lanval is delighted to accept, and the two enjoy an afternoon of lovemaking in the lady's pavilion. But first she lays this requirement on Lanval:

> *"Friend," she said, "now I entreat you, and warn you most urgently, that you do not reveal our love to anyone! And I shall tell you the reason for this: if our love is made known, you will have lost me forever; you will never be able to see me again, or have possession of my body."*

(Marie de France, *Lanval*, ll 143-150)

Later on the handsome young knight catches the eye of Queen Guinevere, who more or less commands him to become her lover. Lanval refuses, on the grounds that he will not be a traitor to his liege lord, King Arthur. The Queen then loses her temper, and accuses Lanval of being a despiser of women:

> *"Lanval," said she, "well I know that you care nothing for such delights; and people have told me often enough, that you have no desire for women. Truly, you have been well-taught, you and those you waste your time with."*

(Marie de France, *Lanval*, ll 277-282)

This painting by the celebrated illustrator Walter Crane is one of several late Victorian interpretations of John Keats' poem "La Belle Dame Sans Merci." It expresses the sinister and destructive nature of women who ensnare unsuspecting men into sexual obsession with their beauty.

*This illustration from a fifteenth century ballroom manual from northern Italy shows a gentleman dancing sedately with two rather haughty ladies. It shows the public, correct, courtly aspect of a lover's behavior.*

The Queen's accusation of homosexuality so enrages Lanval that he retaliates by declaring that he does in fact have a mistress, and moreover, one so beautiful and noble that the least of her maidens is lovelier and more virtuous than the Queen. Enraged, the Queen reports his scornful words to the King, who is very angry with Lanval and wants to condemn him to death. But Lanval's recent generosity has gained him a lot of friends at court, and they insist on a fair judgment. A day is set by which Lanval must produce his mistress, so that everyone will be able to judge whether he was lying about her beauty. Lanval knows that though he spoke the truth he will never be able to prove it, because by rashly blurting out the existence of his mistress he has lost her forever. And so it proves: despite his tears and entreaties, she refuses to appear or even speak with him. Just as the judges are about to pronounce a sentence on him, however, the lady relents. She rescues her lover by appearing at court and revealing in person how far she surpasses the Queen in beauty.

Absolute loyalty was always a quality much prized in heroes, but in the literature of love the loyalty is applied to the lady, whereas in previous epic literature the bond of loyalty between lord and vassal superseded any other claim. This kind of faithfulness is understood in a very literal way by Andreas Capellanus. He cites in his Rules of Love that:

> III: *No one can love two people at the same time.*

> XII: *A true lover does not desire the passionate embraces of anyone but his beloved.*

> XXIX: *A man who is troubled by excessive lust does not usually love.*

Andreas elaborates on that last point as follows:

*A great excess of lust prevents love, because there*

*are those who are so enslaved to their sensual desires that they cannot be bound in the nets of love; men who, after they have set their minds on one woman, or even taken their enjoyment with her, when they afterwards see another woman immediately desire her embraces, and then are oblivious to the indulgences they received from their first love, and are not grateful for them. Men like this lust after every woman they see indiscriminately. The love of such men is like that of a shameless dog. In fact I believe they should be compared to asses; for they are moved only by those qualities which show men to be just the same as the other beasts and not by those true qualities which set us apart from animals by the difference of reason.*

In romances there are many examples of lovers going to great lengths to be physically faithful to their beloved: for instance, Tristan in the tale of Thomas de Bretagne marries Iseult of the White Hands because she has the same name as his lost love, Iseult the Fair of Cornwall, but cannot bring himself to consummate the marriage. Fenice, the heroine of Chrétien de Troyes's early romance *Cligès*, fakes her own death in order to avoid marriage to a man she hates, so that she can be true to her lover Cligès. Fenice haughtily distinguishes herself from such unfaithful lovers as Iseult the Fair, who was unfaithful to her lover Tristan in that she was occasionally obliged to sleep with her husband King Mark. But there is often a sense too that physical fidelity is only one aspect of a larger fidelity, which embraces truth to one's word, reliability and personal honor.

A true lover is constant in his affections to the point of obsession—there simply is not room in his nature for more than one great love. This is why Andreas Capellanus says in his Rule XXX:

*A true lover is continually and without interrup-tion obsessed by the image of his beloved.*

The concentration is immoderate—and it is only in this aspect of a lover's character that he ought to differ from the rational, polished, discreet manners of the courtier—and in romances it leads to some comically bizarre behavior on the part of lovers who have fallen into a trance-like state of meditation on their ladies.

In Wolfram von Eschenbach's great masterpiece *Parzifal*, for example, the hero is riding along on a winter's day, with the ground covered with snow. Near him a falcon wounds a wild goose, and three drops of blood fall on the snow. Parzifal is transfixed by the sight, because it reminds him of the red-and-white complexion of his beloved wife Condwiramurs:

*And thus he mused, lost in thought, until his senses deserted him. Mighty love held him in thrall.*

Unfortunately, Parzifal has frozen in his saddle with his spear held erect—an attitude expressing a hostile challenge—while in a nearby meadow King Arthur and his knights are encamped. A page brings them news of a knight nearby waiting to joust, and Sir Segramors, followed by Sir Keie, both hasten out to joust with Parzifal. He is oblivious to their challenges until some accident removes the drops of blood from his line of vision, and his trance is interrupted. He then responds with fury, unhorsing both knights, and flinging Keie to the ground with such violence that his right arm and left leg are broken. After each encounter Parzifal simply returns to his contemplation of the blood on the snow. Happily the next knight to appear is the quick-witted Sir Gawain, who, realizing that Parzifal is in a love-trance, brings him gently out of it by draping a yellow scarf

over the drops. Parzifal is then able to converse like a rational person.

Chrétien de Troyes' romance *Lancelot* demonstrates the tenets of courtly love better than any other. In it, we find the hero once again almost incapacitated by his obsession. Sir Lancelot, with other knights of the court, has set off in pursuit of Queen Guinevere, who has been abducted by the wicked knight Sir Meleagant. The first night Lancelot and Gawain

*An illustration from a late fourteenth century devotional treatise showing three knights returning from a tournament.*

lodge together in a town and in the morning Lancelot sees from a window a procession of people including a tall knight leading a beautiful lady on horseback:

> *The knight at the window recognized that it was the Queen. As long as she remained in his sight, he continued to gaze at her most attentively, and with delight. But when he could see her no longer, he wanted to fling himself out of the window and shatter his body on the ground below. He was already halfway out of the window when my lord Sir Gawain spotted him and pulled him back in. "Sir, for heaven's sake, calm yourself!" he said. "For the love of God, never think of doing such an insane thing again! You are very wrong to hate your own life thus."*

A little later on Lancelot finds a comb by the roadside with several golden hairs caught in its teeth. Informed that the comb and hairs belonged to Queen Guinevere, he seizes the hairs:

> *... he began to adore the hairs; a hundred thousand times he touched them to his eyes, his mouth, his forehead, and his cheeks. His joy was made manifest in every way, and he thought himself rich and happy indeed. He placed the hairs in his*

*breast, close to his heart, between the shirt and the skin. He would not exchange them for a cartload of emeralds and carbuncles ...*

This careless disregard for worldly wealth is also characteristic of the quality of generosity. It is a quality inherited from the hero of earlier epic poetry, when a warrior's worth was rewarded by gifts of gold and valuables from his lord. In the world of courtly love the lady inherits the loyalty the hero formerly gave his lord; generosity in theory is mutual, but in practice, since the lady is often much richer than her lover, she also inherits the lord's traditional openhandedness. But all lovers must be generous, and must never be mean or miserly. Andreas thought this important enough to include it in his Rules of Love:

(Book I rules:)

1. *You shall flee from Avarice as from a noxious plague, and you shall embrace its opposite.*

(Book II rules:)

10. *Love can never dwell in the house of Avarice.*
26. *Love can deny nothing to love.*

This generosity does not take the form of merely giving gifts to the beloved, though that of course is not a bad thing, but it is also seen as giving general gifts—charity to the poor, hospitality to strangers, honoring friends, and helping those in trouble. We see this in operation in the anonymous Breton lay *Graelent*. The hero, like Lanval, has become the lover of a very rich woman, who has given him unlimited access to her wealth. With it he first pays off all his debts, then gives a great feast; he helps many poor knights in difficult circumstances through war, and releases prisoners. He collects men-at-arms, sergeants, squires, so that he can go to war or to the tournament properly equipped and supported. He also collects clerks, minstrels and heralds, so that he can entertain nobly. He gives all these people gifts of clothing, horses, arms; he earns himself a reputation for being a most liberal, openhanded knight.

Courtesy in the Middle Ages meant much more than just being polite. It also entailed being debonair, witty, sensible, clever, and kind. It meant knowing the right thing to say on each occasion, and never being rude, aggressive or boorish. These qualities had to be cultivated and carefully balanced in a lover, of course; but the quality of courtesy, the polished good manners of the courtier, are to some extent at variance with some of the more emotionally unbalanced aspects of love. The character in romance who embodied courtesy above all else was Sir Gawain. In the romances of Chrétien de Troyes, Gawain is always preeminent, the best knight of the Round Table, but he always appears as a good friend, kind and generous to his fellow knights and welcoming and helpful to strangers, in contrast to the rude and sarcastic Sir Kay. We see him, for example, ever ready to pledge his service to ladies, giving away an expensive horse to Sir Lancelot in *Lancelot*, attempting to restrain the King from doing rash things which will result in discord in *Erec et Enide* and *Lancelot*; and in *Yvain* (or *The Knight with the Lion*) reaching a pinnacle of courtesy after his combat with Yvain. In this romance Yvain and his cousin Gawain have each undertaken, without the other's knowledge, to do battle on behalf of two sisters quarreling over a disputed inheritance; and neither is wearing his usual arms. They fight all day, until both are badly wounded and utterly exhausted. Each then confesses that he has never met so good a knight as the other, and would gladly know the name of his opponent. When they learn one another's identity, and that each has been doing his best to kill the man he loves most in the world, they throw away their swords and shields, and are reconciled. Then Gawain tells the King that Yvain has beaten him. Yvain protests that it was he who was defeated, and each tries to concede victory to the other, until King Arthur compels them to abide by his decision.

But, though he excelled at the social virtues which unite in courtesy, both towards his fellow knights and towards ladies, Gawain was always too well-balanced to be overwhelmed by passion. He appears in medieval romance as rather a ladies' man, but he has no one great love to transform his life. For other knights, however, love was an inspiration which enabled them to achieve excellence.

With noble joy commences
The verse, which rhymes fine words,
And is without a flaw;
But it does not seem good to me that the sort of
person
Who is not fit for my song should learn it.
For I do not want a vile singer,
The sort who would spoil any song,
To turn my sweet ditty into braying.

Of love I have the recollection
And its fair speech; but it does not give me more
than that.
But by patiently waiting
I hope that some joy will come to me from it.
The secular life demands that one behave like this,
Because it can always happen
That in a short time circumstances improve
So that you have plenty of what you hungered for.

I have a fair seeming from her outwardly,
So that she greets me and speaks with me
courteously;
She makes no concession to me of anything more,
Nor is it meet that I should aim so high,

Or that such rich joy should befall me
As would become an emperor.
She does a great deal just to speak kindly to me,
And permit me to love her.

She makes me feel very afraid
For she gives away so little of herself;
Joy that like this is too shrinking
Does not show much encouragement.
Let her retain me if it pleases her,
As long as she does not make me suffer such great
pain;
It is not for me to reproach her,
For she does not keep me so painfully bound.

Without sin I have done penance,
And it is wrong that she does not pardon me;
And I have for a long time desired
The sort of pardon that she does not grant.
I do believe that evil will befall me,
For a man in despair is lost.
By Our Lord I make claim,
Let me have some good hope.

Peire d'Auvergne

# CHAPTER FOUR

## JOURNEYING, SEEKING AND SUFFERING

ORTH is an important concept in courtly love. The knight seeks worth, to enhance his reputation in the eyes of others. His worth—fame for his deeds and for his ability to exemplify the qualities discussed in the last chapter—will enhance that of his lady; her worth—her beauty, virtue, and social status—will also enrich him. This is well expressed in a lyric poem by the famous German minnesinger and jouster, Ulrich von Lichtenstein:

*Knights who seek for honor, you should make sure*
*Of serving when you're armed ladies of worth:*
*If you wish to use your time*
*In knights' ways, with honor,*
*Pay court to fairest women.*

*Your courage should be high as you bear your shield;*
*You should be polished, bold, blithe and gentle*
*Serve knighthood with all your skill*

*And be glad, set love high,*
*Thus shall you win high praises.*
*Think now of the greetings of great ladies,*
*How sweet they make the life of their dear friends.*
*He who wins ladies' greetings*
*Wins honor, his desire;*
*His joy is all the sweeter*

Andreas Capellanus does not mention the performance of heroic deeds in service of the beloved in his treatise, but this is principally because he is aiming to show that the skillful use of words is the way to a woman's heart. Even he, however, is quite clear that it is only a good character and excellent reputation that make a person worthy of love. He has nothing but contempt for anyone who pays too much attention to their looks in order to attract the opposite sex:

*A beautiful figure attracts love to itself with little effort … A wise woman therefore will seek to match herself with the kind of man whose character is praised for integrity, not one who anoints himself all over like a woman, or is immersed in the cult of the body. And just as we have stated this about men, so too we believe that in women not beauty so much as excellence of character should be sought after.*

(Andreas Capellanus, *De Arte* Book I, chapter VI)

But in other courtly literature it was an accepted part of a lover's lot, his apprenticeship in the service of love, as it were, to win renown for his lady's sake. This is where the bizarre ethos of courtly love fits most snugly with the sterner demands of chivalry. The knight who aspired to win a lady's love was motivated to achieve. Thus Troilus:

*The deeds of combat, sharp and deadly storms,*
*That Hector and his brothers undertook,*
*Stirred him no longer as they had before,*
*And yet was he, on horseback or on foot,*
*Among the best, who longest did remain*
*Where danger was, and such great feats performed*
*That all who saw him marveled and admired;*
*But not for any hatred of the Greeks*
*Nor even for the rescue of the town,*
*Did he this warrior frenzy daily seek,*
*But lo, only for this conclusion—*
*To please his lady more with his renown.*
*To such effect in battle he appeared*
*That unto death the frightened Greeks him feared.*

(*Troilus and Criseyde,* Book I, ll 470-483)

Ambition for love's sake is rare nowadays, when it is more usual to crave achievement for the sake of personal satisfaction—and when it is also less acceptable for ladies to acknowledge openly that they would rather have lovers who are successful and famous! But it was expected then, at least in the world of courtly love. A classic example of the reasoning that love improves the character of the lover by giving him something to strive for is to be found in the Middle English *Guy of Warwick*. We have seen how Guy confessed his love to his lord's daughter Felice and was rejected, and how he returned a second time, careless of the consequences, to faint at her feet. When he recovered, Felice informed him that:

*Another fifteenth century representation of knights jousting. The knowledge that he was being watched by his beloved encouraged the knight. Success at this sport could lead to fame and riches and success in love; failure could mean financial ruin and humiliation.*

*No man may I love, to speak right,*
*Unless he be a noble knight;*
*Fairness and courage he must have,*
*Be strong in arms and thereto brave;*
*When you have promised arms to bear,*
*And I have understood it here,*
*Then you shall have my love—so far*
*As you show yourself what I think you are.*

(*Guy of Warwick,* ll 667-674)

Felice has perceived that Guy has the potential to be a truly great knight, famous throughout the world for his strength, nobility, and prowess. Guy thinks she means that she will grant him her love if he gets knighted. He duly hurries back to court to persuade Earl Rohaut to knight him, then returns and claims Felice's love. Felice informs him that he has only the name of knight; he must now go and earn himself a reputation that shows him to be worthy of it. Guy spends a year traveling round Europe attending tournaments, winning the prize at each, gaining friends and a reputation for courtesy, generosity, and prowess. At the

*A very intimate moment is portrayed in this late fifteenth century German painting of two lovers. The young man gazes tenderly at the lady while she admires his jewel. Opposite: The unusual contortion in this German carved wooden figure of a mummer dancing in a carnival parodies the polished politeness of the courtly lover.*

end of a successful year, Guy returns to claim Felice's love. But he has done just well enough to show how much better he could do if he really applied himself, and Felice declares that she cannot bear to hinder him from fulfilling his potential:

> You are not yet so praised that I
> Cannot find others praised more high.
> True, you are strong, and have great might,
> A good chevalier and bravely fight,
> But if I should now grant you my love,
> While we both live, to hold and have,
> You would succumb to idle sloth;
> To take up arms you would be loath.
> Your knightly honor would ruined be,
> If I let you remain with me.
>
> (Guy of Warwick, ll 1132-1146)

So poor Guy has to set off once more on his travels. This time he graduates from taking part in tournaments to participating in real battles and fighting for real causes. In the course of these he achieves great fame, becomes renowned as the best knight in the world, no one can stand against him, and eventually he succeeds in gaining Felice's love.

This episode reflects one of the great concerns of medieval romance, and one of the paradoxes so beloved by medieval people: that the best knight, having won the fairest lady, will quickly cease to be the best knight, because the enjoyment of his successful love will destroy those very knightly qualities which drove him to achieve excellence. This problem forms the basis of Chrétien de Troyes' romance Yvain.

Yvain, having won the love of the lady Laudine and married her, is tempted away by his cousin Sir Gawain to attend tournaments and perform deeds of arms, because, Gawain explains:

> What? Would you become one of those men who are worth less because of their wives? May the man who gets married only to degenerate be shamed by the blessed Mary! Anyone who has a beautiful woman for his wife or lover ought to be the better for it, for it cannot be right that she should love him after he has lost his fame and his worth … Now more than ever it is of the first importance that your worth should increase!… Now you must not idle your time away, but you must frequent the tournaments, engage in combat, joust hard, whatever it costs you!… It is amazing how you can acquire a taste for an easy life, if you live it for any length of time. But pleasures grow sweeter by

*In the late Middle Ages it became customary to present an award to the knight who was judged to have excelled at the tournament. This exquisite painting by René d'Anjou shows his queen about to award a valuable jewel as the prize.*

*delay, and it is far better to taste a small pleasure that has been postponed, than a great one that can be enjoyed today.*

(Chrétien de Troyes, *Yvain*, ll 2484-2518)

Yvain is at last persuaded to leave his new wife and go on the tournament circuit with Gawain. Laudine agrees to this, on condition that Yvain returns to her in a year and a day. But Yvain enjoys himself so much in the company of Gawain and the other knights that he forgets to return at the appointed time, and loses Laudine's love. Though rarely expressed in such terms now, this conflict between love and ambition, or love and the other parts of one's life which need expression, is felt just as keenly, and probably causes even more broken relationships than ever it did in medieval romance.

The final aspect of the tasks a lover must perform to be worthy of his lady that we should look at is the concept of submission to her will. The adage which forms the basis for Chaucer's *Wife of Bath's Tale*—that what women really

(Book II rules:)

5. *A lover will not enjoy anything he does that is against the will of his beloved. (NB. This can also be interpreted as: "If a lover takes his beloved against her will, he will not enjoy it.")*

25. *A true lover considers nothing good but what he thinks will please his beloved.*

26. *Love can deny nothing to love.*

Chrétien de Troyes' *Lancelot* provides the most searing example of this rule put into practice. During the course of his attempt to rescue Guinevere from her abductor Lancelot is compelled to ride in a cart, something which, Chrétien assures us, was considered very disgraceful in those days, as only criminals ever

want is to have sovereignty over men—is taken for granted in the world of courtly love. Andreas Capellanus formulates the following rules:

(Book I rules:)

7. *Being obedient to the commands of ladies, you shall always be eager to attach yourself to the service of love.*

*In order to discover where his beloved Queen Guinevere has been taken by the wicked Sir Meleagant, Sir Lancelot is forced to endure the humiliation of riding in a cart normally only occupied by criminals on their way to execution.*

rode in carts on their way to be executed. Lancelot hesitates before entering the cart, reluctant to bring shame on his rescue attempt, but as this is the only way in which he can learn where the Queen has been taken, he gets in. He then suffers constant shame and ridicule from everyone he meets, as "the knight of the cart," and undergoes all kinds of danger and suffering, including crawling on his bare hands and knees over a bridge made from the blade of a sword, before doing battle with the wicked Meleagant for the Queen's freedom.

Lancelot defeats Meleagant, then disarms himself and hurries to present himself to the Queen. She refuses to speak to him or even look at him. Not surprisingly, Lancelot is dumbfounded; sorrowfully leaving the court, he concludes that she hates him because he rode in the cart. Later, after fearing one another dead, the lovers are reconciled, and Lancelot then learns that Guinevere's former cold behavior was a punishment, not for riding in the cart, but for hesitating to get into it.

He had put his knightly reputation before her safety for two seconds—not good enough by the Queen's exacting standards!

Later in the romance Lancelot attends a tournament in disguise and, at first, fights like a prodigy, as a man should who wants to impress his beloved. The Queen recognizes him and sends him a message that he is to "do his worst." Obediently, Lancelot misses his opponents, and then runs away from them, till all the other knights despise him for a coward. All day and all the following day Lancelot is forced to obey the Queen's instruction—a complete inversion of the normal striving to win in order to please the lady and bring her honor. It is also a much keener test of Lancelot's love for Guinevere, since it contradicts his self-love. Eventually Guinevere is satisfied that Lancelot is sufficiently humble and obedient, and tells him to do his best, and he then fights so magnificently that he wins the prize.

When the days are long, in May,
The sweet songs of birds from far away sound lovely
to me;
And when I have left them behind,
I call to mind my love from far away;
Then I go forth so shadowed and downcast
That neither song nor whitethorn blossom
Can do any more for me than frozen winter.

Well, I hold that lord to be true
Through whom I shall see that love from far away;
But, for each good that falls to me from it,
I have two ills, for I am at such a distance.
Oh! Why am I not there as a pilgrim,
So that my staff and my cloak
Could be noticed by her beautiful eyes.

Distressed and grieving I shall depart,
If I do not see that love from far away.
I know not whether I will ever see her,
For our lands are so far apart;
There are enough roads and passes,

It is not for that reason that we are divided -
But all shall be as she pleases!

Never shall I rejoice in love again,
If I do not enjoy that love from far away,
For I know of none nobler or fairer than she
In any place, either near or far;
So great and supreme is her worth
That there in the kingdom of the Saracens
I would for her sake be claimed captive.

Jaufré Rudel

# CHAPTER FIVE
## THE CONJUNCTION OF THE MIND, AND THE OPPOSITION OF THE STARS

**S**HAKESPEARE remarked that "the course of true love never did run smooth." In the literature of courtly love this is as true as it is in life, or rather more so, because it was recognized that tales of true love that do run smooth do not necessarily make interesting stories. In the medieval world of courtly love it was a truth universally acknowledged that absence made the heart grow fonder, and that familiarity bred contempt. The cynical Andreas Capellanus recommended a few difficulties in love affairs to keep the interest alive, because lovers whose desires are unthwarted will become bored. He agreed with all other writers on the subject when he declared in his Rules that love was intensified by frustration:

(Book II Rules:)

14. *Love easily obtained is of little value; difficulty in obtaining it makes it precious.*

And later on, when Andreas is talking about the ways in which love once fulfilled may be intensified, he elaborates:

> *First of all it is said to improve if the lovers can only enjoy the sight of one another and come together infrequently and with difficulty; and in fact the greater the difficulty in standing before one another and embracing one another, the greater the longing, and the more the desire for love grows … love is usually intensified if you have gone away, or are about to go away, and also by the tirades and floggings that lovers endure from their parents. For not only does a beating or a strict sermon make a love already brought to completion grow greater, but it can also cause the springing up of a love not yet begun.*

(Andreas Capellanus, *De Arte,* Book II, chapter II)

A delicate balance had to be maintained for, as he went on to explain, love is diminished by lovers seeing one another too often and spending too much time in one another's company, since every appetite fades with excess.

How could lovers ensure that their affections could be wrought to a feverish pitch of intensity by difficulties and frustrations? Andreas mentions the interference of disapproving parents, and this indeed was a prime source of fruitful separation for the lovers of medieval romance. Parental interference came in many guises in the literature of courtly love. For instance, the parents of one lover object to their son's or daughter's choice because they are of inferior social status—something which of course matters not at all to people in love. In the strange Old French *Aucassin and Nicolette*, for example, Aucassin's father, the Count Garin de Beaucaire, objects to his son's loverlike behavior because he is completely neglecting his chivalric duties.

Aucassin thereupon confesses that he is not behaving like a good and valiant knight because all he wants is to be with Nicolette. His father is outraged at hearing this, because Nicolette is a nobody. She was brought from a distant country as a child captive, and was purchased from Saracens by the viscount of the town, who later adopted her as his daughter. He will doubtless find some good man with a decent job to marry her honorably, but she is no concern of Aucassin's; he ought to marry the daughter of a king, or of another count. Aucassin declares that Nicolette is so beautiful and noble that she is worthy to be Empress of Constantinople or Germany. When Count Garin perceives that he cannot argue his son out of love with Nicolette, he decides to remove her altogether, and bullies her adoptive father into locking her up in a high tower with only one small window—a favorite way of keeping ladies out of the paths of their lovers in medieval literature.

In the anonymous prose *Suite de Merlin* we hear a similar story. Merlin recounts to Nimue the story of two faithful lovers:

*Not a hundred years ago, there lived in this country a king called Assen, a noble man and a good knight, who had an excellent and valiant knight for his son, named Anasteu. He loved the daughter of a*

The Persian Queen in her Tower. Miroir de l'Humaine Salvation, *fifteenth century, Flanders.*

Regina psaru contemplat̄ pīnaz de orto

57

*poor knight with a greater love than mortal man has ever felt for a woman. When King Assen learned that his son had cast his love so basely, he was very angry and said, "If you do not stop seeing her, I shall have her killed!"*

Before the king could carry out this threat, his son and the lady eloped and spent the rest of their lives in hiding in a remote part of the forest. Similarly, in the Old French poem *Floris and Blanchefleur*, Floris' father, who is a Saracen, threatens to have the Christian captive Blanchefleur put to death because his son has fallen in love with her. Dissuaded from this cruel course by his Queen, he sells Blanchefleur to foreign merchants, but it loses him his son as well, because Floris instantly sets off in pursuit of his beloved when he learns what has happened.

A less common example of paternal obstructiveness can be found in Marie de France's lay *Les Deuz Amanz*, in which the King

William Bell Scott's painting *Fair Rosamund Alone in her Bower. In real life Rosamund Clifford was the mistress of King Henry II of England, who visited her in a bower at the center of a labyrinth to protect her from the jealous fury of his wife, Queen Eleanor.*

of Normandy was so very fond of his daughter (especially since the death of his Queen) that he could not bear anyone to marry her and take her away from him. The king of Normandy sets his daughter's suitors an impossible task—to climb, unaided, to the top of a very high mountain carrying his daughter in their arms. No one can succeed in performing this task, and until the hero of the lay comes along they have given up trying.

But more common still than parental interference in medieval romance is the interference of jealous spouses, especially husbands. It was quite a cliché of the genre for a beautiful young woman to be married off to an older man who, riddled with jealousy and desperate to keep his treasure to himself, locks her up in an impregnable tower. Invariably the effect of this behavior is to make the lady in question determined to betray her husband with the first man clever enough to find his way inside. This happens to the luckless heroines of the Breton lays *Guigemar* and *Yonec*, the Provençal poem *Flamenca*, and the Tristan romances, to name but a few. The early Tristan romances are a very good example of the efficacy of opposition in maintaining love, because in some versions it is the jealous attempts of King Mark to entrap the lovers and keep them apart that heightens the obsession felt by Tristan and Iseult for one another. In Béroul's *Tristan*, when they have eventually fled the court and gone to live in pastoral bliss in the forest, they tire of their love after a few years and split up voluntarily!

But, no sooner have they been recalled to King Mark's court, than the restraints imposed on them by the suspicious King rekindle their passion:

> Hearts and eye go traveling along the paths that have always brought them joy; and if anyone attempts to spoil their game, he only makes them the more passionate about it, God knows.... so it was with Tristan and Isolde. As soon as they were forbidden their desires, and prevented from enjoying one another by spies and guards, they began to suffer intensely. Desire now seriously tormented them by its magic, many times worse than before; their need for one another was more painful and urgent than it had ever been.

(Gottfried von Strassburg, *Tristan und Isolde*, ll 17,828-17,947)

Gottfried follows this with an entertaining reflection on women's morals, arguing that keeping a woman locked up or under surveillance is the surest way to drive her to commit adultery, even if she was very virtuous before, because it is in the nature of women :

> Women do lots of things just because they are forbidden, which they would certainly not do if they were not forbidden.... Our Lord God gave Eve the freedom to do what she would with all the fruits, flowers and plants there were in Paradise, except for only one, which he forbade her to touch on pain of death.... She took the fruit and broke God's commandment...but it is my firm belief now that Eve would never have done this, if she had not been forbidden to.

A typical case occurs in the Provençal romance *Flamenca*. At the beginning of the poem the lovely Flamenca is married to the great Lord Archimbaut, who loves her passionately. But the Queen of France's envious gossip causes him to suspect Flamenca, and he works himself into a jealous rage, furious with every man who so much as looks at her. To prevent her from being seen at all, he locks her up in a tower. His insane jealousy is the talk of the country, and everyone sympathizes with the terrible plight of the young and beautiful girl shut away in the tower. Although Flamenca has married Archimbaut out of obedience to her father, she has been prepared to love him, but his treatment of her makes her unhappy and resentful.

When at last her situation comes to the ears of the young William of Nevers, he falls madly in love with her (although of course he has never seen her).

William contrives to disguise himself and take the place of the priest whose task it is to hand Flamenca the wafer of Holy Communion each week—the only time she is seen at close quarters by any man other than her husband.

Each week he is able to say only two words to her, but by six meetings they have arranged an assignation. Among the lovers spurred on to bolder deeds by the difficulties placed in their way, a good example is the hero of Chrétien de Troyes' *The Knight of the Cart* (Lancelot). When Lancelot and Guinevere have at last been reconciled with one another after a series of misunderstandings, they wish to speak in private. The Queen is being kept a virtual prisoner in the castle of King Bademagu—for her own protection, to keep the wicked Sir Meleagant away from her—and she warns Lancelot that they cannot be together physically. The door of her chamber is kept locked and guarded night and day, the badly wounded Sir Kay is sleeping in her bedchamber, and its windows are protected by thick iron bars:

Page 61: The Death of Tristan *by Marianne Stokes.* Above: *A fifteenth century illustration from the* Prose of Lancelot, *showing Lancelot and Guinevere's first embrace, achieved by the diplomacy of Lancelot's friend Galehalt, almost under the very noses of the queen's ladies-in-waiting.*

When Lancelot perceived the Queen leaning towards the window at the massive iron grille, he greeted her in a low voice. The Queen returned his greeting, for she greatly desired him, as he did her. In their words was nothing base or disagreeable, on the contrary. They drew as close to one another as they could, and held each other's hands. They were maddened beyond endurance at not being able to come together, and they cursed the iron bars. But Lancelot boasted that if the Queen consented, he would enter the chamber; it was not the bars of the window that were preventing him. The Queen said, "Do you not see how solid these bars are—how could you break them, or even bend them...?" "My lady," answered Lancelot, "do not think of that! The iron is worthless as far as I'm concerned. Nothing will stop me from coming in to you, but you yourself. If you grant your permission, the way is free. But if you do not wish it, then the path is so full of obstacles that I shall never be able to pass."

"As for me, I desire it," said the Queen. "My wishes will never prevent you..."

...the knight prepared himself to attack the window. He grasped the bars, heaved and pulled them down until he had quickly bent them all and could force them out of their sockets. But the iron was so sharp that it pierced the tip of one finger to the bone, and sliced through another at the first joint. But his preoccupation was so intense that he felt no pain from these wounds, nor did he notice the blood which poured from them.

(Chrétien de Troyes, *Lancelot*)

The undoubted psychological truth of Andreas' rule that difficulty in obtaining love makes it more precious probably contributed to his less justifiable insistence that love can only exist outside marriage. The modern equivalent of this medieval equation of love with adultery, is the excitement derived, exactly as Andreas prescribes, from its infrequent meetings, achieved with difficulty, ever in fear of discovery.

Glorious king, true light and radiance
Almighty God, Lord, if it pleases you,
Be a faithful helper to my friend;
For I have not seen him since the night came over,
And soon it will be dawn.

Fair friend, whether you sleep or wake,
Sleep no more, but softly rise again;
For in the East I see the star risen
Which leads in the day, and well I recognize it;
And soon it will be dawn.

Fair friend, I call you in my song,
Sleep no more, for I hear the bird sing
As it flies searching for the daylight through
the woods,
And I am afraid that the jealous one may
attack you;
And soon it will be dawn.
Fair friend, go to the window,
Look at the stars in the heavens!

You will know that I am a true messenger to you.
If you do not, it will be your loss,
And soon it will be dawn.

Fair sweet friend, I am staying in such a
wonderful place
That I wish the dawn and the day would never come,
For the most beautiful creature that ever a
mother bore,
I hold and embrace, and therefore I care nothing
For the jealous fool, or for the dawn.

**Giraut de Borneil**

# CHAPTER SIX

## A CONSUMMATION DEVOUTLY TO BE WISHED

A T last, after all the difficulties and tribulations, separations, obstacles, and the anguish of unrequited love, the lovers can finally come to an understanding. At the first opportunity the lovers surrender themselves to the absolute bliss of that special, exclusive private world of personal happiness that makes all the pains endured to achieve it seem worthwhile.

The troubadours expressed themselves eloquently on the subject of love, but in terms which make it clear that their views and goals varied widely. The work of the first troubadour whose poems have survived, Duke William IX of Aquitaine, dates from about 1100, and there can be little doubt of what the goal of love should be in his opinion. Occasionally his celebration of the charms of his mistresses can be extremely coarse:

*Two horses I have to my saddle, fine and noble:*
*they are good, skilled at arms, and valiant; but I*
*cannot keep them both, for one of them hates the*
*other.*

*If I could only tame them to my will, I would*
*never want to put my equipment in any other*
*place, for I would be better mounted than any man*
*alive.*

*Knights, give me your counsel for this problem!*
*I was never more perplexed by a dilemma; I don't*
*know by whose side I should stay, by that of the*
*Lady Agnes, or that of the Lady Arsen.*

Even when he expresses his delight with more charm and delicacy, however, we are left in no doubt that his love for the lady is far from platonic:

*I'll make a new ditty, before the wind, the ice,*
*and the rains come; my lady tests me and puts me*
*on trial to discover how, in what manner, I love*
*her; but not for any action she could bring against*
*me would I ever free myself from her bonds.*

*Instead I surrender and yield myself up to her,*

so that she can write me into her charter; and don't think I'm a drunkard if I love my fair lady, for without her I cannot live, I have such a great hunger for her love.

For she is whiter than ivory, and therefore I adore no other. If I do not have help soon, to make my fair lady love me, I will die, by the head of St Gregory! If she does not kiss me in her bedroom, or outdoors.

Other poets vary. The troubadour Bernart de Ventadour's verses addressed to Duke William's granddaughter Eleanor of Aquitaine were so scorching that they gave rise to a general belief that Bernart and Eleanor had been lovers in real life, not just in the fantasy world of courtly love:

> I have placed my good hope well, since she whom I most desire and yearn to see shows me her beautiful face: frank, gentle, noble and faithful, in whom the king would be saved, beautiful and

graceful, with a lovely body, she has made me from nothing into a rich man.

> …Ah, my good and longed-for beloved, with well-formed figure sweet and slender, with fresh, pretty colored skin, whom God made with his own hands! Always I have desired you, and no one else pleases me—I want no other love.

And again:

> If I knew how to cast spells on people,
> My enemies would be children,
> So that no one could ever discover
> Or tell a thing that could do us harm.
> Then I know that I would see that most lovely lady,
> And her beautiful eyes and her fresh complexion,
> And I would kiss her on the mouth again and again,
> So that the mark of it would show for a month.
> I would like well to find her alone,
> While she slept, or made semblance of it,
> So that I could steal a sweet kiss from her,
> Since I am too unworthy to ask for one.
> By God, my lady, we accomplish little of love!

This belief received support over the years from

the extraordinary reputation enjoyed by Eleanor in the Middle Ages as a scandalously emancipated woman. Eleanor was extremely intelligent, cultured, witty, able, energetic and decisive, as well as being beautiful. She was married to the pious King Louis VII of France in 1137 at the age of fifteen. After fifteen years of marriage, she had produced only two daughters, and in 1152 she dared to divorce Louis, on the grounds of consanguinity. Within eight weeks, to the scandal of Europe, she had married the young prince Henry of Anjou, who was twelve years her junior (and a much closer blood relation than Louis had been!). Henry was the heir to the throne of England as well as all his father's lands in Anjou, and when these were united with Eleanor's vast territories in the southwest of France, he became lord of the biggest empire in medieval Europe. Eleanor bore five sons and three daughters to the virile Henry, but the marriage was not a success in other ways; the couple became estranged after a few years, and led virtually separate lives. Eleanor spent a lot of time in France in her own territories, where she was joined by her daughter Marie, now the Countess of Champagne. Together they presided over courts

Opposite: *A miniature portrait of Bernart Ventadour, whose humble origins did not prevent him from writing love poetry for Eleanor of Aquitaine. Later scholars supposed them to have been lovers.* Above: *Aristocratic marriages, especially among the great nobles and royal families, were almost always arranged for political and economic reasons, as in this fanciful sixteenth century portrayal of the marriage of the Emperor Frederick III and Eleanor of Aragon.*

of dazzling sophistication and were notable patrons to many poets and musicians.

Because so much is known about Eleanor's life, it is tempting to speculate on the question of how real the love between her and Bernart was. Though there are many excellent reasons for deducing that the love between Eleanor and Bernart was strictly romantic and literary, there is no proof that they were not lovers in the real sense. It should be remembered that courtly love was partly conceived as an imaginative escape from the horrors of a loveless marriage. It is therefore allowable to hope that Eleanor, both of whose marriages were miserable, at least experienced the happiness of personal fulfillment in the arms of her favorite troubadour.

For other poets, it is clear that they reject physical consummation and wish to lead the concept of courtly love to its logical conclusion, as a totally idealized relationship, in which the quasi-religious veneration of the lady could not possibly be sullied by anything so crude as lust. Such refinement, however, is conspicuously absent in Andreas Capellanus. He coyly refers to the joys experi-enced by lovers as *solatii* ("solaces") which could cover the whole spectrum from rampant sexuality to saintly and chaste devotion; but it is clear from instructions to the young initiate into the secrets of love, Walter, to whom the work is ded-icated, that he intends the "solaces" to be under-stood in a thoroughly physical way. He says, for example, that clerics ought not to seek love, because they are bound to renounce all the plea-sures of the flesh and keep themselves pure and unspotted for the Lord's service; similarly, men ought never to seek love from nuns, because it is unholy and forbidden and leads to eternal damna-tion. In romance, there are less descriptions than you might suppose of the bliss of physical union. Of course you would not expect to find descrip-tions of ladies and knights actually making love in twelfth century literature, but you would expect

Opposite: *An illustration from the famous French allegorical poem "Le Roman de la Rose," in which the lover dreams of being able to pluck the jealously guarded Rose. In this scene, he has been allowed into a garden belonging to Sir Mirth and his wife Lady Gladness.*

to find the kind of eulogy briefly given by Chré-tien de Troyes in *Lancelot*:

*The Queen stretched out her arms to him and embraced him; she pressed him to her breast, and then drew him into the bed beside her. She made him the most beautiful welcome that anyone could do who was inspired by love in their heart. Indeed, she felt for him great love, but Lancelot loved her a thousand times more. Love had taken root in his heart so completely, that there was scarcely any left over for other hearts. Now Lancelot had everything he desired; the queen wished him to stay beside her and enjoy her; he held her in his arms and she held him in hers.*

*Their blows were so gentle, so sweet, that through their kisses and caresses they experienced a joy and wonder the equal of which has never been known or heard of. But I shall be silent on this subject, for it should never be recounted; for the rarest and most delectable pleasures are those which are hinted at, but never told.*

(Chrétien de Troyes, *Lancelot* )

The reason why you do not often find purple passages on successful love is that romances often tend to dwell more on love thwarted than love achieved. Of the examples that are to be found in romance, however, even the most euphemistic have a powerful erotic charge:

*When she knew who William was, it gave such great joy to her heart that she utterly abandoned herself to him. With her arms about his neck, she kissed him, and nothing now can frighten her away from her desire to serve him, to kiss him, to caress him, and to do all that Love wills. Neither eyes nor hands nor lips were still; they kissed one another ardently and clung together, nor did they try to conceal their passion. And they acted so as to reach the peak of joy between them.*

(*Flamenca*, ll 5934-5946)

Opposite: *On this illustration from a medieval manuscript Tristan and Isolt innocently drink the love potion.*

*That night, as the beautiful girl lay pining and yearning for her beloved, her lover, Tristan, and her doctor, Love, stole into her cabin together.*

*Doctor Love led Tristan, her sufferer, by the hand, until she found there her other patient, Isolde. Then she seized both the suffering ones and gave them to one another, to be their mutual cure. Whenever there was a suitable opportunity, they seized their fill of what lovers long for. Throughout the whole voyage they were in ecstasy.*

(Gottfried von Strassburg, *Tristan*)

The poet of passion fulfilled par excellence, however, is Chaucer, whose moving account of the first night spent together by Troilus and Criseyde cannot fail to impress the most hardened cynic:

*Criseyde, quite free from every dread and fear,*
*Like one who had good cause to trust in him,*
*Made such fair welcome, it was joy to hear,*
*When she knew all his faith and pure intent;*
*And as sweet honeysuckle's shoots are sent*
*Curling and wreathing round a stately tree,*
*To wind and bind him in her arms can she.*

*Her tender arms, her back full straight and soft,*
*Her slender flanks, all fleshly, smooth, and white*
*Now he began to stroke, and blessed full oft*
*Her snowy throat, her breasts full round and light,*
*Thus in this heaven taking his delight;*
*And many thousand times he kissed her too,*
*Scarcely—from joy—knowing what next to do.*

*Of all the joys they had, one of the least*
*Is out of my capacity to say;*
*But you, if you have tasted such a feast,*
*Judge of their gladness, their sweet amorous play;*
*I can say nothing more than these two*
*That night, between certainty and dread,*
*Began to learn Love's power and worthiness.*

*Oh blissful night, that they so long had sought,*
*How blithe unto the two of them you were.*

*Why had I such one with my soul not bought,*
*Yea, or the least joy that was there?*
*Away, foul danger, and away, you fear,*
*And in this heavenly rapture let them dwell,*
*That is more lovely than my tongue can tell.*

(Chaucer, *Troilus and Criseyde,* Book III, ll 1226-1407)

No medieval person would seriously consider that a night of joy like this was worth losing one's soul for, and in fact both Chaucer and Andreas Capellanus published retractions of their apparently immoral writings on love; but the magic of the glittering, illusory world of courtly love is that it can make a night of bliss seem worth anything.

But in courtly love as in life, no goal is achieved in order to create a static period of happiness. Another goal appears behind it; for love is always either increasing or decreasing (says Andreas) and, once the lovers have achieved their union, their blissful togetherness, how are they going to keep it?

*Opposite: A composite illustration from a fifteenth century manuscript of Troilus and Criseyde, showing them in bed on the first night in which they consummate their love.*

I have heard the sweet voice
Of the wild nightingale,
And it has leapt into my heart
So that all my woes
And the evil blows that Love has given me,
It soothes and heals.
And another's joy could help me well
In my grief.

A false, wanton traitress
Of low descent
Has betrayed me, and is herself betrayed,
And cuts the stick with which she beats herself.
And when someone else exhorts her,
She accuses him of her own crime.
And the last ones [to arrive] get more from her
Than I, who have waited for her so long.

I served her very nobly,
Until she revealed her fickle heart to me;
And since she has not been gracious to me,
I would be a great fool to serve her any longer.

Service that is not rewarded,
And the Bretons' hope *
Make a squire of a lord
By custom and usage.

Since she is so faithless towards me,
I shall leave her dominion
And I do not want her anywhere near me,
Nor do I seek ever to speak to her;
But yet if someone talks to me about her,
The speech makes me feel better,
And I willingly rejoice in it,
And it lightens my heart.

God grant an evil fate
To him who brings bad tidings!
For I would have had the joy of love
If it had not been for false tell-tales.

Bernard de Ventadour

* [i.e. that Arthur would return]

# CHAPTER SEVEN

## THE GREEN-EYED MONSTER

ONE way in which the medieval lore of courtly love departs from our modern perception is in its positive attitude to jealousy. Jealousy can be a terrifyingly destructive emotion, it is an inevitable byproduct of passion. Even in the mannered world of the courtly lover, jealousy was considered an indispensable part of love. Andreas recorded in his Rules that *"He who does not feel jealous is not capable of loving."*

Writers on courtly love were never judgmental about jealousy, regarding it as one more symptom—a major one—of the disease of love. We have been taught differently, and have become accustomed to the idea that love should be selfless, and that the true lover thinks only of their beloved.

We regard jealous love as wrong, something to be avoided, something to be ashamed of; but the Middle Ages, with perhaps a more ruthless recognition of the facts, simply knew that

jealousy was inseparable from romantic love, and codified it along with the rest.

Andreas Capellanus has much to say on the subject of jealousy. For him, fear is an ever-present part of love, and jealousy is bound up with this. He sees love as a most evanescent phenomenon, and defines its state in his Rules as one of permanent flux:

> 4. *It is well-known that love is always either growing or declining.*
>
> 17. *A new love drives out the old.*
>
> 19. *If love lessens, it soon fails and rarely recovers.*

In view of this, it is no wonder that according to Andreas lovers are always on the lookout for signs of waning affection in their partners, and are quick to interpret any little want of attention as a sign that they have lost their beloved to someone else. This is not a sign of monstrous egotism, but of insecurity and vulnerability—something all lovers are subject to. In his Rules he points out that:

20. *A man in love is always fearful.*
21. *The feeling of love is always increased by true jealousy.*
22. *When a lover feels suspicious of his beloved, jealousy, and with it the sensation of love, are increased.*
28. *A small supposition compels a lover to suspect his beloved.*

We feel little sympathy for the sort of love which according to Rule XXVIII makes a lover ready to suspect their partner of infidelity on the flimsiest of evidence, but note how Andreas talks of true jealousy as if there is a good and a bad kind. He explains in his discussion of how love can be increased after it has been consummated, that jealousy can be as useful as hardships and difficulties as a strategy for increasing love:

> *Love also increases, if one lover shows himself to be angry towards the other; for the other lover will at once be violently afraid in case this angry spirit of their loved one should last permanently. And also,*

*Love's Passing by Evelyn de Morgan illustrates the moment which is, according to Andreas Capellanus, inevitable in all love affairs.*

*love is very much increased when one of the lovers is in the grip of true jealousy, which indeed is called the nurse of love. In fact, if a lover is laboring not under true jealousy, but under unworthy suspicion, even so love is known to become more powerful by virtue of this feeling... But also, if you know that someone is working to turn your lover away from you, this will without any doubt increase your love, and you will begin to feel greater affection for her.*

(Andreas Capellanus, *De Arte*, Book II, chapter II)

He gives an account of the distinction between true jealousy and unworthy suspicion in the dialogue between the nobleman and the gentlewoman. The nobleman says:

*For true jealousy is a passion of the soul, through which we are terrified that the substance of our love may be diminished by some failure to observe the wishes of our beloved, and it is an anxiety about the inequality of love, and it is suspicion of one's beloved, but without any unworthy*

*thought. From this it is apparent that there are three kinds of jealousy. A truly jealous man is always afraid that his services will not be good enough to retain for himself the love of his beloved; and that she will not love him as much as he loves her; and he is compelled by the tormenting pain of jealousy so much that he wonders whether his beloved is embracing another lover, even though he believes that such a thing is completely impossible.*

(Andreas Capellanus, *De Arte*, Book I chapter VI, dialogue 7)

In other words jealousy is an unworthy suspicion when it is founded on a conviction of the beloved's infidelity, but it is true jealousy when it is founded on a conviction of the lover's own unworthiness. It is an emotional response to anxiety experienced in defiance of rational thought. In this sense jealousy has a wider meaning in courtly love than it has today; it does not refer solely to jealousy of other people, but to anything which might cause the loss of the beloved's affections.

There is something uncomfortable and

hypocritical about the rules and definitions of Andreas, as if he is advising would-be lovers to ape the behavior of people who are in the grip of uncontrollable passion, merely in order to give their own more tranquil feelings a specious sincerity. For the courtiers reading Andreas' treatise, with their controlled and disciplined lives, set in rigid hierarchies and regulated by powerful customs, the idea of suffering the terrible agonies of jealousy may even have seemed attractive. But when we come to the poetry of love, and to the romances, this sense of counterfeiting passion fades away, and we are faced with the real griefs, torments, doubts and quarrels of medieval lovers.

In the poems of the trobairitz we find verse on jealousy from the angry and outspoken:

> *Elias Cairel, I want to have the truth*
> *About the love you and I once had,*
> *So if you please, tell me truthfully,*
> *Why you have given it to someone else.*

> *For your songs do not sound as they once did,*
> *And yet I did not save myself for one day from you,*
> *Nor did you ever demand such love of me*
> *That I did not place myself entirely at your*
> *command.*

> *Elias Cairel, you are false and feigning,*
> *And you seem to me to resemble*
> *A man who pretends to have an illness*
> *When he has not, and feels no pain at all.*
> *If you would believe me, I would give you*
> *good counsel:*

> *Turn back into a monk,*
> *And do not dare ever to speak of me,*
> *But in your prayers to the Patriarch Ivan.*
> *If you please, Elias, I would like*
> *You to tell me who your new lover is,*
> *So tell me, and have no fear,*
> *That I may judge her worth and qualities.*

> (Isabella)

to the purely hurt and sorrowful:

*I do not wish to sing, and yet I must;*
*So bitter do I feel towards my friend,*
*For I love him more than anything else alive;*
*He does not value my pity or courtliness,*
*Nor my beauty, nor my fame, nor my intelligence.*
*I have been cheated and betrayed,*
*As if I were utterly vile and worthless.*

*It is a marvel when your heart hardens*
*Towards me, my friend, and therefore I have reason*
*to grieve;*
*It is not right for another love to take you from me,*
*For anything she can say or promise.*
*Remember what it was like in the beginning*
*Of our love! God forbid*
*That I should be to blame for the ending of it.*

(Countess of Dia)

Queen Guinevere was one of the most jealous and demanding of lovers in medieval romance. We have already seen how she rejects Lancelot in Chrétien de Troyes' *The Knight of the Cart*, just for hesitating two seconds before undertaking public humiliation in the course of his attempt to rescue her. In later romances this queenly rejection of less than perfect behavior in her lover was developed into a whole personality dominated by jealous insecurity, and by the time of Sir Thomas Malory's *Le Morte Darthur* Guinevere had been long established as a tormented person, whose moods swing between passionate tenderness and appalling cruelty. Here we see her in the final part of the tale, accusing the long-suffering Lancelot of not loving her any more:

*Upon a day, she called Sir Lancelot unto her chamber, and said thus: "Sir Lancelot, I see and feel daily that your love begins to fade, for you have no joy to be in my presence, but ever you are out of the court, and nowadays you have more matters and quarrels for ladies and gentlewomen than ever you used to have before."*

*Beautiful maidens trapping men's hearts in a net is from Pierre Sala's*
Emblèmes et Devises d'Amour, *a collection of French love poems.*

[Lancelot defends himself at length, to no avail. He implores her to understand that he is trying to amend his life, and at the same time to divert the suspicions of talebearers in the court.]

*All this while the Queen stood still and let Sir Lancelot say what he would. And when he had said all, she burst out weeping, and so she sobbed and wept a great while. And when she could speak, she said: "Lancelot, now I well understand that you are a false cowardly knight, and a common lecher, and you love and hold other ladies, and you have nothing but disdain and scorn for me... now I understand your falsehood, know that I shall never love you more. And never be so bold as to come in my sight; I discharge you from the court, that you never come within it; and I forbid you my company, that you never see me again, on pain of your head." Right so Sir Lancelot departed with great heaviness, that scarcely he might sustain himself for great sorrowing.*

(Sir Thomas Malory, *Le Morte Darthur*, Book XVIII, chapters I and II)

Fortunately for Lancelot, it soon becomes necessary for the Queen to recall him when she is wrongly accused of murder, and no other knight will defend her in a trial by combat.

In other romances, we find that lovers' quarrels are caused by jealousy of the knight's pursuit of prowess just as often as by jealousy of a human rival. Chrétien de Troyes was the preeminent poet of this conflict between romantic love and the quest for fame. In his *Yvain* the hero leaves his new and adored wife Laudine at the persuasion of his friend and cousin Sir Gawain, to take part in tournaments. She releases him on condition that he return to her in a year and a day. But Yvain is having such a good time on the tournament circuit that he forgets his promise until the day is past and it is too late. Laudine withdraws her love, and sends Yvain a message via a maiden:

*She thus entered the pavilion, and came directly before the king. She told him that her lady saluted him, and my lord Gawain, and all the others except Yvain, the disloyal traitor, the liar, the impostor, who had deceived and deserted her.*

*"Well has she perceived his falsehood, who made himself out to be a true lover, but was a traitorous, deceitful thief. My lady was deceived by this thief, when she did not suspect any evil, and by no means expected that he would steal away her heart... The true lover, wherever he may be, holds his lady's heart dear and brings it back again. But Yvain has caused my lady's death, for she believed that he would look after her heart and return it to her when a year had passed. Yvain! You were very forgetful, that you couldn't remember that you had*

*to return to my lady within the year... My lady occupied herself in her chamber by counting the days and seasons ... her complaint does not come without reason or before its time; I raise no cry against him for anything but this—that he betrayed us, when he married my lady. Yvain, my lady cares for you no longer, but she commands you by me, never to return to her, and no longer to keep her ring."*

(Chrétien de Troyes, *Yvain*, ll 2714-2770)

Yvain has to suffer many pains and hardships before he is reconciled with his lady and enjoys redoubled happiness.

Notice how all these examples assume that jealousy will have a positive effect. It is very serious, but it reminds us of Andreas' advice that jealousy is a useful tool for keeping love at a pitch of vivid intensity. The more violent the quarrel, the sweeter the reconciliation, and the more tested, the truer the love. This is all very well for those whose stories end happily. But what about the love affairs that go horribly wrong?

Opposite: *The first kiss between Lancelot and Guinevere. From a thirteenth century manuscript.*

I do not sing for a bird or a flower,
Nor for snow nor for ice,
Nor even for cold or warmth,
Nor for the return of the green to the meadows;
Nor for any other pleasure
Do I sing, nor have I ever sung,
But for my lady for whom I long,
For she is the fairest in the world.

Now I am parted from the worst
That ever was seen or found,
And I love the most beautiful lady in the world,
And the most highly prized.
And this I shall do all my life –
That I shall be the lover of no other lady;
For I believe she feels good will
Towards me, or so it appears to me.

Truly I shall have great honor, my lady,
If ever you grant me such a privilege
That under the bedcovers
I might hold you naked in my arms;
For you are worth the hundred best ladies,
And I'm not exaggerating to say so.
My heart rejoices only in this worth,
More than if I were emperor!

I make of my lady my lord and my mistress,
Whatever destiny may bring,
For I have drunk of love,
So that I must love you, in secret.
Tristan, when noble Yseult the Fair granted him
[love],
Was unable to do anything else,
And I love through such a covenant
My lady, and I cannot escape from it.

You see, lady, how God helps
The lady who takes pleasure in love:
For Yseult was in great fear,
Then quickly she was counseled
How she should make her husband believe
That no man born of woman
Had ever touched her before: and now
You can do exactly the same!

Carestia, some joy
Bring me from that dwelling
Where is my lady, who holds more joy for me
Than I know how to tell.

Raimbaut d'Orange

# CHAPTER EIGHT

## THE FATAL PASSION:

### LOVERS WHO RUN MAD OR DIE FOR LOVE

ANDREAS Capellanus not only acknowledges that love affairs can go wrong, but declares it to be inevitable that they will in his Rules of Love:

4. *It is well-known that love is either growing or declining.*

18. *A new love drives out the old.*

29. *If love lessens, it soon fails and rarely recovers.*

With this built-in obsolescence in mind, he devoted considerable space in his treatise to advising lovers on what to do if they think that their love affair is going stale. In the case of a woman who has fallen in love with someone and subsequently finds that he has been unfaithful to her, Andreas advises:

*... if a woman wishes to keep a wavering lover,*
*she must take pains to keep him in the dark about her plans, and to conceal her inmost thoughts and feelings, and she should show him by careful simulation that her spirits are not affected by the disturbance in their love, but she must pretend for all she is worth to tolerate calmly and patiently whatever her lover does. But if the woman realizes that no progress is being made by this contrivance, she should very cautiously pretend that she is thinking of the embraces of another man, so that her lover, remembering those rapturous favors which he used to enjoy so eagerly before, and thinking that they are now being shown to someone else, may feel pangs of jealousy, and may begin to long for those favors with all his heart. But if by these strategies the lost love cannot be recovered, the wisest advice which can be given to a woman is, to try to forget this man, and to avoid the memory of his love.*

(Andreas Capellanus, *De Arte,* Book II, chapter VI)

Other examples too show that Andreas expected lovers to regulate their behavior according to the rules and precepts laid out in his treatise, and had little sympathy for those whose feelings ran away with them. Passion was an unpardonable excess for Andreas; he felt some sympathy for lovers who were suffering the agonies of disappointment and rejection, but in the final analysis, love should be a manageable passion, which must always be subdued to better judgment.

In real life then as now, the advice to lovers to get the better of their feelings and forget partners who have betrayed them was impossibly hard to put into practice. While great achievements have been inspired by succesful love, it is also true that disappointed love can result in terrible tragedies and crimes. In medieval romance love appears a much more stern and terrible driving passion, and lovers who are disappointed, betrayed, or rejected, often run mad or die.

The archetype for the lover who runs mad seems to be the original Tristan romance. This was composed in about 1150, and has not survived, but an anonymous later fragment derived from it describes Tristan's madness:

> Tristan had already suffered such grief on behalf of Yseult, that he was really insane... After he had crossed the sea he landed in Cornwall, and swiftly left the seashore. He did not want anyone to think he was sane, so he ripped his clothes, scratched his face, cut off all his blond hair, and hit anyone who got in his way. On the seashore nobody thought he was anything but mad, for they did not know what was in his mind. He held a staff in his hand, and walked along like a fool. All the people shouted at him and threw stones at his head, but he carried on without stopping. For many days he walked through the country in this manner, for love of Yseult.

Later romances copied such details as the torn clothing and cropped hair, but portray the madness as genuine, the result of an unbearable

Opposite: The Madness of Sir Tristram *by Sir Edward Burne-Jones (1862)*

emotional crisis. Thus Chrétien de Troyes describes Yvain's response to being told that because he has not kept his promise to return to his wife Laudine by the appointed day he has forfeited her love and will never see her again:

*Yvain could not answer, for sense and speech failed him ... and his agony grew without ceasing; everything he heard increased it, and everything he saw, it all tortured him. He wanted to flee all alone to a wilderness, where no one would know him, or seek him, where no man or woman dwelt, where no one could get news of him any more than if he had been in the abyss of hell.... He would rather go insane than not to be able to take vengeance on himself, who had robbed himself of his own happiness. He slipped away from among the barons; for he was afraid that he would run amok in front of them.... He went so fast that he was soon a long way from the tents and pavilions. Then such a great storm broke in his head that he went out of his mind; he tore his clothes to shreds, and ran off through plowed fields and meadows, leaving his people wondering what had become of him.... And so he lived in the forest, like a man completely wild and crazy.*

(Chrétien de Troyes, *Yvain*, ll 2774-2828)

And in later prose romances Sir Lancelot has a very similar experience after being tricked into going to bed with the lady Elaine, daughter of the King of Corbenic. When Queen Guinevere hears that Lancelot has been unfaithful to her, even though it was unintentionally (Lancelot had been drugged and thought he was in bed with Guinevere), she reacts with fury and forbids him ever to see or speak to her again:

*"False traitor knight that you are, look you never abide in my court, and avoid my chamber, and be not so bold, you false traitor knight that you are, that you ever come in my sight!"*

*"Alas!" said Sir Lancelot; and with that he took such a sorrow at his heart at her words that he fell down to the floor in a swoon. And with that Queen Guinevere departed. And when Sir Lancelot awoke out of his swoon, he leapt out at a baywindow into*

*a garden, and there with thorns he was all scratched in his face and body; and so he ran forth, he knew not where, and was a wild and crazed as ever a man was; and so he ran for two years, and never might any man have grace to recognize him.*

(Sir Thomas Malory, *Le Morte Darthur*, Book X, chapter VIII)

Opposite: *A fourteenth century illustration of Lancelot driven mad by the conflict between his passion for the queen and his devotion to purity* Above: The Lover and his Lady. *From the* Roman d'Artus, *fourteenth century.*

But these lovers, though they suffer greatly, are the lucky ones; though temporarily bereft of reason, they are eventually cured and reconciled with their beloved. Less fortunate are the literary lovers who can only respond to the pain of betrayal and loss by dying. Again, there was an archetype: Dido, the tragic Queen of Carthage, who in Book IV of Virgil's *Aeneid* fell in love with its hero Aeneas and, when he was forced by the gods to leave her in order to fulfill his destiny of founding Rome, kills herself. This story was adapted in c. 1140 into one of the earliest medieval romances, and Dido became the first of many romance heroines to kill herself for love. She persuades her sister to help her to heap up all the clothes and gifts given to her by Aeneas, in the pretence of wanting to burn them, but intending to make them into her own funeral pyre:

> She was all alone in her chamber, and there was
> no one to prevent her from the misdeed she wished
> to do. She went to draw the Trojan's sword; when

*This painting by Baron Pierre-Narcisse Guerin depicts the moment that seals the fate of Dido, the tragic queen of Carthage. Aeneas tells her the story of the destruction of Troy, as she comforts his young son Ascanius.*

he gave it to her, he never dreamed that she would lose her life by means of it. She took the naked sword and placed the point under her breast; together with the blow, she leapt into the pyre, which her sister had made for her. She lay, face downwards, upon the Trojan clothes and robes on her bed; she writhed and wallowed in her blood. She spoke thus in her agony: "... Alas, that I saw him who gave these things to me, for like a fool I loved him too much, and it has turned to a great misfortune for me. Upon these clothes I want to end my life, and upon this bed where I was shamed; thus I leave my barons and my kingdom, thus I abandon Carthage without an heir, thus I lose my good name, and all my glory, but I shall not die forgotten, for I shall be spoken of through all time. ... He has killed me by the great wrong he has done me; but I forgive him my death here and now; in the name of peace and accord, I kiss his garments and his bed. I forgive you, Lord Aeneas." She kissed the bed and all the hangings; they were all drenched with her blood. She lost the power of speech; her breath came in grievous pants and sobs,

*as death tortured her, and she sighed heavily in her*
*great pain; then her breath failed her completely.*

(Anon, *Le Roman d'Eneas,* ll 2025-2076)

Dido took destiny into her own hands; there
is no doubt of her absolute intention to kill
herself, when the pain of continued existence
became too great to bear. But there were many
other ways than plain suicide to die from love.
In Marie de France's tragic lay *Les Deuz Amanz,*
it is the hero's desire to impress his beloved
that causes his death. In order not to lose his
precious daughter the King of Normandy, the
heroine's father, imposes on her prospective
suitors the impossible task of climbing up a very
steep mountainside carrying her in their arms.
The King's daughter, however, falls very much
in love with the son of a squire, far below her
in rank. She proposes to get from her aunt, a
skilled physician from Salerno, a drug which

*Alexandre Cabanel's painting of* Francesca da Rimini and
Paolo Malatesta, *the tragic couple encountered by Dante*
*in the Second Circle of Hell.*

*Sir Edward Burne-Jones'*
*famous painting* Laus
Veneris *(Praise of Venus) is*
*drawn from another tale of*
*fatal love, the German*
*legend of Tännhauser.*

will artificially increase her lover's strength, enabling him to perform the task and win her hand legitimately. Watched by the King and court, the young man sets off up the mountain with his beloved in his arms, asking her to take charge of the potion—he will drink it when his strength is failing:

*He set off with her at top speed, and climbed until he was halfway up the mountain. Because of the joy he felt from being with her, he forgot to think about his drink. She felt that his strength was failing: "My love!" she said, "now take your drink! I know you are growing weaker; drink and recover your strength!" But the young man replied: "Fair love, my heart is full of strength; I shall not stop for anything, not even so long as to take a drink, so long as I am able to go three paces more. These people shouting out distract me with their noise, and it hinders me. I do not want to stop here." When he had climbed two-thirds of the mountain, a puff of wind would have blown him over. Over and over the maiden begged him: "My love, drink your medicine!" He did not want to hear or believe her. A terrible anguish filled him. He reached the top of the mountain, and felt such agony that he fell down, never to rise again; his heart had burst in his breast.*

(Marie de France, *Les Deuz Amanz,* ll 180-205)

The damsel then dies of a broken heart, holding the dead body of her beloved clasped in her arms. Such unbearable grief is understandable in human terms, even when it has become a literary convention; but even more extreme reactions are experienced by other medieval heroines. The heroine of the anonymous *La Châtelaine de Vergi* has for her lover a noble knight, who had sworn to her never to reveal their love to anyone, in accordance with the traditional requirement of secrecy. The wife of his overlord the Duke then made advances to him and, on being rejected accuses him to her husband of attempting to seduce her. The Duke forces the knight to reveal his love for the Châtelaine de Vergi. He asks the Duke not to reveal the identity of his love to anyone; but the spiteful Duchess finds out and tells the Châtelaine that her lover has

been boasting about her. The Châtelaine, distraught, seeks solitude in her chamber, where she bewails the supposed faithlessness of her lover:

*"When I granted him my love freely, I told him and made this agreement, that the moment he made our love public, he would lose me. Now we must part, and I cannot live with this bitter sorrow; and if I could, I would not want to. Life is worthless; I pray to God therefore to grant me death, and to have mercy on my soul. As I have truly loved him who has caused my death, I forgive him the wrong he has done me, and pray to God to honor and protect him. Death is not so bitter if it comes to me through him; and when I remember his love, I am happy to die for his sake." After this, the châtelaine spoke no more, except to sigh: "Sweet friend, I commend you to God." Saying this, she crossed her arms before her breast. Her heart burst within her, and her face lost its fair hue. In her agony she fainted, and fell back on the bed, pale and discolored, without life or breath.*

(Anon, *La Châtelaine de Vergi*)

She dies of a broken heart, convinced that her lover had betrayed her trust and no longer loved her. Soon her faithful knight comes looking for her and, finding her dead, thrusts a sword into his own heart.

Love in person could also strike down a lover. The *Knight's Tale* tells such a story. The two young heroes, Arcite and Palamon, have to fight a formal battle to determine who shall win the hand of Emilia. The night before the battle the practical Arcite prays to Mars, God of War, to grant him victory. Palamon, on the other hand, prays to Venus to give him Emilia, whatever may happen in the battle. Sure enough, Arcite wins the battle, but as he is savoring the moment of victory, Saturn at Venus' request sends a spirit to frighten Arcite's horse; he falls, suffering fatal chest injuries. As he lies dying, very far from intentionally, he utters this lament:

> *"Alas, the woe, alas the pains so strong,*
> *That I for you have suffered for so long!*

> *Alas, the death! Alas, my Emilie!*
> *Alas, the parting of our company!*
> *Alas, my heart's own queen, Alas, my wife!*
> *My heart's dear lady, ender of my life!*
> *What is this world? What can men ask to have?*
> *Now with his love, now in his cold grave,*
> *Alone, bereft of any company."*
> (Chaucer, *The Knight's Tale*, ll 2771-2779)

Even more cruel is the fate in store for poor Troilus, whose agony on learning that his beloved Criseyde has been faithless, and has begun a liaison with Diomede, is so painful that death seems a blessed relief. Troilus seeks death in battle, and eventually finds it when he encounters the almost invincible hero Achilles.

Of course, it is to be hoped that then and now, lovers who lose their beloved for whatever reason will eventually find peace through healing time or a new love, but there have always been the unhappy few for whom nothing but a rejection of life itself is a sufficient cure for the pain of lost love.

The firm desire which enters my heart
Cannot be torn from me by the beaks or nail,
Of a tell-tale, even if he arms himself to speak evil;
And since I do not dare to beat him with a staff or cane,
At least by stealth, there where I have no uncle,
I will rejoice in joy, in the pleasure-garden or in the
    bedroom.

When I remember the bedroom
Where, to my grief, I know that no man enters,
But they are all worse to me than her brother or her uncle,
I have not one limb that is not trembling, or one
    fingernail,
More than a child does before the cane;
Such terror I feel that my soul is too much hers.

Would I were hers in body, not in soul!
And that she would consent to hide me in her bedroom!
For it wounds my heart more than the blows of the cane,
Because her servant may not enter there, where she is;
I shall be with her just like her flesh or her fingernail,
And I shall not fear the rebuke of her friend or uncle.

For like this my heart clings and hangs on with its nail
To her as the bark clings to the cane;
For she is to me the tower, the palace, the bedroom of joy,

And I love her more than any cousin or uncle.
Then in paradise my soul shall have a double joy,
If ever a man enters there through good loving.

Arnaut sends forth his song of the fingernail and the uncle,
For the pleasure of her who arms him with her cane,
To his heart's desire, who enters worthily her bedroom. *

Arnaut Daniel

*(N.B. Arnaut invented a new form, the sestet, for this poem, which is incredibly clever though the translation reads rather strangely. In the original, every line of every stanza ends with one of the same six words: intra (enter), ongla (fingernail), arma (arm in the sense of put on armor, or soul), vergua (cane), oncle (uncle) and cambra (bedroom). In each of the six stanzas these words are in different lines, i.e. the same word is never in the same line twice.)

# CHAPTER NINE

## THE MARRIAGE OF TRUE MINDS

A FURIOUS debate raged in the Middle Ages about the nature of love. Could true love exist within marriage? This is not without relevance today when for many couples matrimony can herald the end of romance. In a sense the whole idea of courtly love developed in response to social circumstances in which marriage was often likely to be loveless—when it was arranged for political or economic considerations. But marriages of affection were not unknown, even in the twelfth century, and for some writers marriage seemed the natural outcome of successful love. Some writers however, saw romantic love as different in kind from the affection between married people.

In the first two books of his treatise Andreas Capellanus maintained his stance on the incompatibility of true love and marriage. In one of his dialogues which details a conversation between a nobleman and a gentlewoman, the lady advances the argument that she ought not to grant him her love because she has a very good and noble husband who loves her with all his heart, and whom she loves in return. This leads to an extended discussion of the possibility and propriety of true love within marriage. The nobleman argues that the affection between husband and wife is not the same thing as true love; while the gentlewoman disagrees with him.

Perceiving that they will never agree, the two of them refer the dispute to the arbitration of the great Countess Marie of Champagne, whose definitive decision is as follows:

> *We state and consider as firmly established, that love cannot exert its powers between two married people. For lovers give everything to one another freely, not by reason of force or necessity. Married people, on the other hand, have to obey each other's wishes out of duty, and can deny nothing of themselves to one another. Besides, how does it*

*increase a husband's honor, if he enjoys his wife's embraces like a lover, since neither of them will be improved in worth and virtue by this, and they seem to possess nothing but what they have always had a right to? And we shall assert yet another reason: for a precept of love informs us,*

*that no woman, even a married woman, can be crowned with the prize of the King of Love unless she is perceived to be enlisted in love's service outside the bonds of matrimony. And indeed another rule of love teaches that no one can be wounded by love for two men. Therefore, Love cannot rightly acknowledge that he has any rights between married people.*

(Andreas Capellanus, *De Arte*, Book I, chapter VI, dialogue 7)

The examples of alleged real-life cases submitted to the judgment of certain eminent ladies also unequivocally support the argument that love is not possible between married people. Andreas

cites three: in the first case, a lady who had a perfectly good lover was subsequently married, through no fault of her own, to someone else, and as a result she avoided her lover and refused to see him anymore. The lover appealed for judgment to the Countess Ermengard of Narbonne, whose verdict, in accordance with the first of Andreas' rules of love, was that the lady's marriage did not constitute an acceptable reason for terminating her love affair:

*Entering into a new union of marriage does not by rights exclude a previous love, unless the woman gives up making time for love altogether, is disposed to love no one at all any more.*

(Andreas Capellanus, *De Arte*, Book II, chapter VII, decision 8)

In the second instance the same noble lady was invited to pronounce on whether the greatest affection existed between married people or between lovers. She gave a masterly response,

Opposite: *A priest joins the hands of a bride and groom in this fourteenth century manuscript illustration of a wedding.* Above: *This fifteenth century Italian painting* A Betrothal *by Jacopo del Sellaio depicts a betrothed couple, a king and queen.*

according to the style of scholarly dispute, that it was not possible to make valid comparisons between things that differ in kind, thus claiming of course that these are two things differing in kind, and saving herself from having to advance an argument in support of that proposition.

The third example is the most outrageous of all:

*A certain knight was bound by love to a woman who was tied to the love of another man, but from her he got this much hope of her love: that, if at some time she happened to be deprived of the love of her lover, then without a doubt she would grant her love to this knight.*

*A short time later, this same woman and her lover were married. The knight then demanded to be shown the fruition of the hope she had given him; the woman however absolutely refused, saying that she had not lost her beloved's love. In this case, the Queen responded as follows: "We do not dare to set ourselves against the opinion of the Countess of Champagne, who set down as her judgment that love cannot exert any power between husband and wife. Therefore we recommend that the lady should make good her promise of love."*

Though we can probably agree that the affection of married people is a different sort of thing from passionate love, this is clearly absurd.

In addition, Andreas Capellanus wrote in the third book of his treatise a retraction of everything he said in the first two volumes. Here he confirms that it is really wicked to pursue love outside marriage, for many good reasons: it is disobedient to God's law, it injures your neighbor to sleep with his wife, it leads to selfishness and alienates all your friends; it causes you to suffer the terrible agonies of jealousy; it makes a man into a slave because he has to be obedient to the whims of his beloved; it makes lovers poor because of the requirement of generosity; it leads to loss of reputation, and to all sorts of serious crimes; and most of all, because it is a mortal sin and leads to eternal damnation. He particularly condemns love for being the frequent cause of broken marriages, and for leading men to kill their wives. He then goes on to speak of the great advantages of a good marriage:

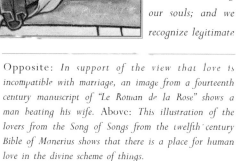

*For a man ought not to love anything in this life as much as the wife to whom he is rightfully and legitimately joined, for God has declared that a wife is one flesh with her husband, and he commanded her, forsaking all others, to cleave to him... Besides, we overcome our lust without sin with a wife, and we remove the incentives to rank excess without staining our souls; and we recognize legitimate*

Opposite: *In support of the view that love is incompatible with marriage, an image from a fourteenth century manuscript of "Le Roman de la Rose" shows a man beating his wife.* Above: *This illustration of the lovers from the Song of Songs from the twelfth century Bible of Manerius shows that there is a place for human love in the divine scheme of things.*

*offspring by our wives, who will offer us suitable comforts both living and dying, and in them God will be able to perceive our fruit.*

(Andreas Capellanus, *De Arte*, Book III)

Which of these completely opposite views are we to take as Andreas' real opinion? Probably Book III, which expresses the genuine disapproval of the medieval churchman for a phenomenon opposed to the laws of the Church, and of the member of an ordered society for something chaotic, powerful, and potentially destructive. His treatise was popular among medieval readers for it was a parody of courtly love pushed to the limits. But Andreas was parodying something real, and there is plenty of evidence from other sources to suggest that his nonsensical arguments about love being impossible within marriage were based on the poetry of the troubadours, and other medieval love literature. In the poems of the troubadours, all the ladies who were the objects of their affections were married, and most were of a

Opposite: *This fifteenth century illustration of the romance of Renaud de Montauban shows the celebrations at the wedding of Renaud and his beloved Clarisse de Gascogne.* Left: *A troubadour playing the lute, from the* Manasseh Codex.

higher rank than their lover; and the most famous of lovers from medieval romance, Lancelot and Guinevere, and Tristan and Isolt, were all in the same classic circumstances, in which a young man has fallen in love with the wife of his overlord. Other romances in which love takes place outside marriage include *Lanval*, *Flamenca*, and *Troilus and Criseyde*. In *Flamenca*, too, the lady is a married woman and the knight is a bachelor. In these circumstances the love affair must be adulterous because the lovers cannot marry one another. This is not the case however in *Troilus and Criseyde*, where the hero is a bachelor and the heroine a widow. There is no obvious reason why Troilus and Criseyde should not simply get married to one another, but

Opposite: *Alfred Carlton Smith's beautiful 1907 painting* The Mandolin. Above: *The poet writing at his desk, from a fifteenth century French manuscript in the Bodleian Library.*

it never seems to occur to them to do this—they just take it for granted that a love affair and not a marriage is the natural sequel to the pains of love. There were nevertheless several romances in which the goal of the lovers was clearly marriage; for example in *Cligès, Yvain, Perceval, Les Deuz Amanz, Guy of Warwick, Floris and Blanchefleur, Aucassin and Nicolette, The Knight's Tale*, and the very interesting *Franklin's Tale*, in which a married lady is approached by a young bachelor knight, but wishes to remain faithful to the husband she loves. The most important of these as a contributor to the debate is *Cligès*, which seems to have been written partly to refute the idea that love within marriage is inappropriate and to provide a specific counter to the popular tale of *Tristan and Yseult*. In *Cligès*, the heroine Fenice has fallen in love with Cligès, but is betrothed to his uncle, the Emperor Alis. Miserably unhappy at the prospect of marriage to a man she detests, she confides in her nurse Thessala, and accounts for her sorrow:

> I would rather be torn limb from limb than that the love of we two should be remembered like the love of Tristan and Yseult, of which so much nonsense is talked that I am ashamed to speak of it. I could not agree to the life Yseult led. Love was too cheapened in her, who gave her whole heart to one man, while two enjoyed the favors of her body. Thus she spent her life, and never refused them both. That love was not rational, but mine shall be constant forever, for nothing will ever cause my heart to go one way and my body another. My body will never be a whore, and two men will never share it. He who has my heart shall have my body; all others I reject.

(Chrétien de Troyes, *Cligès*, ll 3098-3124)

This is a very determined rejection of those precepts of courtly love which dictate that love can only be experienced as something separate from marriage. The same contradiction preoccupies us today. There is nothing so wonderful as to be overpowered by the sweep of romantic love, but everyone acknowledges that after several years of

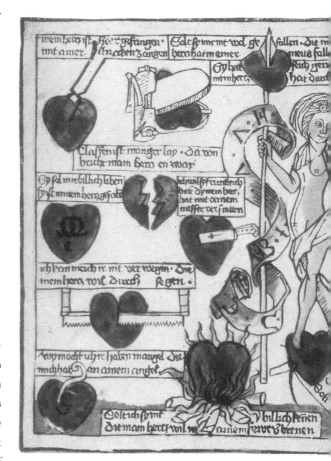

marriage this usually simmers down to a calmer, and ideally more enduring, affection and respect. Thereafter the perilous delights of passion can only be had outside marriage; yet we have been conditioned by our culture to expect that people who are in love with one another will get married, and "live happily ever after" in some effortless way. It is not really very surprising that the middle and upper classes of medieval Europe, untutored in the idea that it is wicked to marry someone you do not love, came up with a system in which marriage was more of a business partnership and nothing whatever to do with love; it is more surprising that we should recognize in so many of the stories in medieval love literature the urge felt by lovers to marry, to celebrate their love in a union blessed by society, and set hopefully forward on a life together.

The Power of Lady Love, an Allegorical Description of the Power of Women over Men's Hearts, *by Caspar von Regensburg. This fifteenth century German manuscript depicts the torments of love with various intruments of torture used on hapless hearts.*

# EPILOGUE

## ROMANTIC LOVE AFTER THE MIDDLE AGES

THE Occitan culture that had nurtured the troubadours was destroyed in the first half of the thirteenth century. In 1209 Pope Innocent III proclaimed a crusade against certain heretical sects who were based throughout the south of France. For the next thirty years war was enthusiastically waged against the people of rich Occitania by the overpopulated and impoverished North; in 1244 the last stronghold of the heretics, the mountain fortress of Monségur, was taken; everyone inside perished. The society, laws, language, and culture of Occitania were smashed forever, and the poetry of the troubadours, which the Church found particularly offensive, was silenced.

But by then it was too late to stop the spread of the religion of love. The troubadours had given voice to something essential, fundamental, deeply rooted. Their view of romantic love had already spread over the whole of western Europe, and it was never to be absent from its literature or from its living consciousness again. The concept of love as obsessive, as a source of insecurity, fear and pain, but yet as potentially yielding the greatest happiness obtainable by human beings in this life, of love as a power for good which refines and ennobles its practitioners, and as something which triumphs over all obstacles—these ideas have become so central to our thought and culture that they seem natural. We scarcely question them or think of them as the direct inheritance of a distant set of historical circumstances; novels and films are still being written and made, nineteen to the dozen, celebrating romantic love.

It seems that people clung to this ideal through all the changes and developments of the succeeding centuries. For, when the Middle Ages faded and were superseded by the sparkling triumphs of the Renaissance, their cultural achievements were thoroughly despised. The cold clear light of classical

Roman and Greek civilization with its reason, philosophy, law, art and architecture, led people to condemn the Middle Ages as a time of barbarism, superstition, and ignorance. Speaking of Sir Thomas Malory's great masterpiece *Le Morte Darthur*, the Elizabethan theorist Roger Ascham memorably commented:

*...the whole of which booke standeth in two speciall poyntes, in open mans slaughter and bold bawdrye: In which booke these be counted the noblest knights, that do kill most men without any quarell, and commit foulest adulteries by subtlest shiftes.*

In the Middle Ages people had inherited a view of their own culture as the poor remains of a more glorious past; thus the splendors of the Roman world were remembered with loving nostalgia in the Dark Ages and beyond. But in the Renaissance people began to look forward with energy and pride, and to see their culture as better than what had gone before, and in a state of calm

*Pieter Breughel the Younger's* Peasants Returning Home from the Fair *shows the playful antics of these robust peasants. There is nothing of the restraint of courtly love in their behavior, but at least they appear to be having fun.*

but continual improvement—an attitude that still prevails today. From the worst excesses of courtly love this new consciousness shrank, appalled. Why should a man make himself the slave of a woman, when he was clearly the superior creature? Why would anyone allow themselves to be dominated by a hopeless, unrequited passion? Why would anyone bring on themselves the misery and guilt of an adulterous love affair? But romantic love, the enduring myth that had sprung from the troubadours and matured in medieval romance, continued to inspire poetry and influence behavior. Even at the height of the Age of Reason, with its distrust of passion and excess, Love was, if not as busy as in the twelfth century, never successfully banished. Men still wooed women courteously, respectfully; they continued to feel that they would be rewarded by her love only after demonstrating their devotion. Literary lovers still found themselves suffering for love, struck by love's darts, slain by beautiful eyes, though they expressed their feelings in new and exciting ways and used the old clichés of medieval romance with tongue in cheek.

But in the final decades of the eighteenth century there was a revolt against reason. The Romantic movement wanted passion, cultivated sensibility, rejected cold logic. At the same time there was a renewal of interest in medieval art and literature, which developed in the first half of the nineteenth century into the great Victorian obsession with medieval culture. Painters like the Pre-Raphaelite brotherhood strove to obtain the massively detailed realism and jewel-like brilliance

*The Game of Chess by Albert Frans Lieven de Vriendt shows a fifteenth century Flemish pair of lovers from the wealthy bourgeoisie.*

and clarity of late medieval art; splendidly elaborate neo-Gothic architecture appeared; books commending the medieval ideal of chivalry reinterpreted for modern times were a great success; the great poets and novelists, notably Scott, Keats, Browning, Tennyson, took medieval subjects for some of their major works. But the Victorians created their own version of medieval ideas. It is principally through the rose-tinted and slightly distorting lenses of Victorian perception that we are familiar today with the concepts of chivalry and courtly love. They brought the nineteenth century's agonized moral consciousness to their subjects, and were far more judgmental than any medieval source. Here, for example, is Tennyson's account of what King Arthur said to Guinevere in their final interview together, after the destruction of the Round Table Fellowship:

*I made them lay their hands in mine and swear*

*To reverence their*
*King, as if he were*
*their conscience, and their*
*conscience as their King,*
*To break the heathen*
*and uphold the Christ,*
*To ride abroad addressing human wrongs,*
*To speak no slander, no, nor listen to it,*
*To honor his own word as if his God's,*
*To lead sweet lives in purest chastity,*
*To love one maiden only, cleave to her*
*And worship her by years of noble deeds,*
*Until they won her; for indeed I knew*
*Of no more subtle master under heaven*
*Than is the maiden passion for a maid,*
*Not only to keep down the base in man,*
*But teach high thought, and amiable words*
*And courtliness, and the desire of fame,*
*And love of truth, and all that makes a man...*
*And all this throve before I wedded thee,*
*Believing, "Lo, mine helpmate, one to feel*
*My purpose and rejoicing in my joy."*
*Then came thy shameful sin with Lancelot;*
*Then came the sin of Tristan and Isolt;*

The last of a set of six tapestries made in Arras, nothern France, in the fifteenth century, and probably intended as a betrothal gift. In this tapestry, "A mon seul désir" (To my one desire) the lady's beloved has sent her a casket of jewels which she is about to put on.

*Then others, following these my mightiest knights,*
*And drawing foul ensample from fair names,*
*Sinned also, til the loathesome opposite*
*Of all my heart had destined did obtain,*
*And all thro' thee!*
(Tennyson, "Morte d'Arthur," *Idylls of the King*)

Medieval authors too had fully appreciated the destructive potential of romantic love, but no medieval person would ever insist on the conjunction of love with chastity and purity.

And so romantic love has come down to us in the final years of the twentieth century, as a consummation devoutly to be wished, and yet fearsomely difficult to obtain. We are brought up from birth with the idea that love makes life worthwhile, that it seductively promises the intensest happiness of personal fulfillment, and that although there may be other reasons for marrying, it is hopelessly wicked to marry without affection. Yet the various pains of disappointment, rejection, jealousy and betrayal are the other side of the coin and cause untold suffering to those unlucky in love. Is romantic love merely an artistic sublimation of sexual attraction? Or is it the expression of something much deeper in the human soul? Is it all an elaborate game, or the true business of life? We leave the judgment in the hands of the reader.

Opposite: *This exquisite fresco of a garden was painted in the first century B.C. for the Empress Livia, beloved wife of the Emperor Augustus. It evokes the peace and natural beauty of the countryside.*

# FURTHER READING LIST

I have trans-
lated almost
all of the
passages quoted in this book, but in most cases
English translations do exist, and for those who
would like to explore the literature of courtly
love further, here is a list of the main texts:

Barron, W. R. J., ed. and trans. *Sir Gawain
and the Green Knight*. Manchester, England:
Manchester University Press, 1974.

*A saintly reader. This early fourteenth century miniature is
the first known representation of someone wearing spectacles.*

Bogin, Meg, ed. and trans. *The Women
Troubadours*. London: Paddington Press, 1976;
New York: W. W. Norton, 1980.

Capellanus, Andreas. *The Art of Courtly Love*.
Introduction, edited text, translation, and notes
by John Jay Parry. Edinburgh: Edinburgh
University Press, 1971.

Chaucer, Geoffrey. *The Knyghtes Tale* and
*Troilus and Criseyde*. In *The Riverside Chaucer*.
Introduction, edited text, and notes by L. D.
Benson. Boston: Houghton Mifflin Co., 1987

Coghill, Nevill, trans. *Troilus and Criseyde*.
New York: Viking Penguin, 1971.

Corley, Corin, trans. *Lancelot of the Lake*.
Introduction by Elspeth Kennedy. New York:
Oxford University World Classics, 1989.

de Troyes, Chrétien. *Arthurian Romances.* Introduction, translation, and notes by William W. Kibler. New York: Viking Penguin, 1991.

Eschenbach, Wolfram von. *Parzifal.* Introduction and translation by Helen M. Mustard and Charles E. Passage. New York: Random House, 1961.

Fedrick, Alan S., trans. *Tristan*, by Béroul, (with an appendix of *Tristan's Madness*). New York. Viking Penguin, 1970.

Hatto, A. T, *Tristan*, by Gottfried von Strassburg, (with an appendix of *Tristran* by Thomas de Bretagne). New York: Viking Penguin, 1960.

Hubert, Merton Jerome, and Marion E. Porter, eds. and trans. *Flamenca*. Princeton, NJ: Princeton University Press, 1962.

Malory, Sir Thomas. *Le Morte Darthur.* Introduction by John Lawlor, edited text by Janet Cohen. 2 vols. New York: Viking Penguin, 1969.

Mason, Eugene, trans. *French Medieval Romances from the Lays of Marie de France.* Everyman's Library. London: J. M. Dent & Sons Ltd., 1911; New York: Dutton, 1911.

Press, Alan R. ed. and trans. *Troubadour Lyric Poetry*. Edinburgh: Edinburgh University Press, 1971.

Schöler Beinhauer, Monica, ed. *Le Roman D'Eneas.* Munich: Wilhelm Fink, 1972.

Zupitza, Julius, ed. *The Romances of Guy of Warwick.* From the Auchinlek MS and the Caius MS. Oxford: Early English Text Society, 1966.

ACKNOWLEDGMENTS

Peasant wedding procession *by Pieter Breughel.*

Mary Evans Picture Library, London: 2, 10, 14/15. Scala, Italy: 9, 67. The Bridgeman Art Library, London: 19, 33, 37, 38, 41, 50, 52, 57, 61, 62, 68, 71, 76/77, 81, 90, 92, 94, 101, 104, 106, 108, 110. Bodleian Library, Oxford: 20/21, 24, 47, 72, 107. Louvre, Paris: 23. Fine Art Photographic Library, London: 29, 58, 113, 114, 122. British Library, London: 30. Gotha Schloss Museum: 48. Stadtmuseum, Munich: 49. Bibliotheque Nationale, Paris: 66. Private collection: 87. Pierpont Morgan Library, New York: 88. Carpentras Bibliotheque (Inguimbertine): 89. Bibliotheque St. Genevieve, Paris: 102, 103, 120. El Escorial, Madrid: 105. Prado, Madrid: 117.

Every effort has been made to trace all present copyright holders of the material used in this book, whether companies or individuals. Any omission is unintentional and we will be pleased to correct any errors in future editions of this book.